D1022790

HIGH
5

"The Truth Project is a no holds barred revelation revealing the investing pornography being fed to the Main Street investor by the Wall Street Bullies. With courage and passion, Wayne gives brilliant insights on how you can ignore the Wall Street lies and glean the real truth that will finally give you the true peace of mind you deserve."

— Mark Matson, Founder & CEO, Matson Money

◆◆◆

"My clients all have a net worth of $20M or more. In reading Wayne's book I noticed that many of my clients (if not all) live the core truths Wayne outlines. For those looking for a way to lead a more rewarding financial life Wayne's book would be a great place to start."

— Scott Hamilton, CEO, InKnowVision LLC

◆◆◆

"I've know Wayne for many years and have always been impressed with his commitment to 'telling it like it is'. Similarly, in this book, he has laid the facts on the table. Every parent and grandparent needs to read this book, and give copies to their children and grandchildren to help each of them prepare for their own successful retirement."

— Susan Bradley, CFP®, Founder, Sudden Money Institute

◆◆◆

"Wayne von Borstel does not mince words; he is honest and ethical, and these characteristics are exemplified through his wisdom in The Truth Project. In my 36 years of experience in the financial services industry as a writer and consultant, Wayne's book is the first I have read that bravely reveals the truth about the 'man and the machine behind the curtain (Oz).' The only book an investor needs to read … ever."

— Sydney LeBlanc, Co-founder Registered Rep magazine

The
TRUTH
PROJECT

Finding the Courage to
Ignore Wall Street

Wayne von Borstel, CFP®, ChFC®, CLU, MSFS

The opinions voiced in this material are for general information only and are not intended to provide specific advice or recommendations for any individual. To determine which investment(s) may be appropriate for you, consult your financial advisor prior to investing.

Securities offered through LPL Financial. Member FINRA/SIPC.

Financial planning offered through Oregon Trail Financial Services, a Registered Investment Advisor.

PUBLISHER
High 5 Communications, LLC
1371 East 150 South
Hyrum, UT 84319
Tel: 435.750.0062
email: info@high5communications.com

AUTHOR
Wayne von Borstel, CFP®, ChFC®, CLU, MSFS
von Borstel & Associates
308 E. 3rd Street
The Dalles, OR 97058
Tel: 541.296.6669
    800.600.6669
email: wayne@vonborstel.com

Print	
(hard cover) ISBN: 978-0-9857797-2-6	Cover Price: $21.95 USD
(soft cover) ISBN: 978-0-9857797-3-3	Cover Price: $15.95 USD

Digital	
ePub ISBN: 978-0-9857797-4-0	Cover Price: $9.95 USD
Mobi™ ISBN: 978-0-9857797-5-7	Cover Price: $9.95 USD

Quantity discounts are available. To purchase, please contact the publisher or the author.

To the three women whose lives have been what my life has become:

My grandma Elsie, for her unrelenting belief and pride in what she knew I was and could become.

My mother who put up with my bad side to help me see my best side.

My wife, who has always been there with what I needed. Without her undying support, comfort and love, nothing I am today would be possible.

Even the simplest of feats is done from many resources never known! So it is with a book. But with heartfelt thanks I want to thank Michael Dubes for believing, listening and pushing. Lyn Fisher for giving me the touch I thought I needed and Mark Matson for the link between what I believed and what I delivered as a financial planner. There are literally thousands who have touched me during the process of coming to what this book represents ... so thanks to all of you and enjoy the "Truth."

As a friend and associate of Wayne von Borstel for more than 10 years, I have deep respect for his honesty and common-sense approach to both his life and his business. In everything he does, Wayne takes a long-term perspective that keeps the focus on goals and outcomes while avoiding the temptation to become distracted by short-term gains.

Through the years, as I have interacted with Wayne at LPL Financial meetings and events, and even spent time socially with him and his wife, Marta, I have come to understand why Wayne has garnered so much respect in our industry. It is equally clear why so many of his clients choose to stay with Wayne year after year, even extending their relationships through multiple generations.

Most importantly, Wayne recognizes the value of looking at a person's total financial life. As a financial planner, Wayne creates a financial roadmap for his clients, one they can follow over their lifetime.

Wayne is a practical person with a clear understanding of what it takes to get through life successfully. Most importantly, he practices what he preaches. Wayne advocates financial concepts that, to some, may initially seem quite simple, and yet these concepts are true and sensible, regardless of whether they are applied by someone who is just starting out or someone who has already accumulated significant wealth. In essence, what Wayne is advocating is a return to fundamental ideas, such as acquiring an early savings habit, spending less than you make, investing for the long-term, and investing only in things you understand. Wayne doesn't just sell investments; he provides peace of mind.

In my career, I've noticed that people sometimes put themselves under tremendous stress when it comes to investing. They chase returns. They spend time worrying about how to pick the right stocks or where to find the next big thing. Wayne understands that, ultimately, the value is in solid planning and asset allocation. He knows that statistical performance is not nearly as important as having a good asset mixture that provides adequate diversification over the long haul. Just as important is having an advisor who understands your goals and continually monitors and periodically rebalances the portfolio to ensure it is optimized to help you achieve those goals. Again, it is a common sense approach that is both prudent and effective.

Wayne has devoted his career to doing what is best for his clients. He is candid and committed to telling his clients what they need to hear. Even when the information may be unpleasant, he states his beliefs and has confidence in his convictions. In the midst of challenging economic times like these, straight talk from a trusted advisor is more important than ever. When times are tough, many people tend to avoid making decisions about reallocating assets because they are unsure what to do. It's a time when emotions, playing an especially large role, can be dangerous.

That's when having an advisor like Wayne is important. People need an advisor who not only knows the right things to do, but is willing to push past emotional reactions and help them follow the plan while keeping a long-term financial perspective. This ability to share frank insights is one of the things I value most in my personal relationship with Wayne, and I am sure he is equally direct with his clients.

The opportunity to partner and work alongside advisors who, like Wayne, genuinely love what they do is one of my greatest joys as a leader of the nation's largest independent broker/dealer. The work they do to help individuals identify goals, address the realities of their financial situations, and plan for the future is as noble as it is vital. I am proud to be associated with a trusted and committed financial advisor like Wayne von Borstel.

CEO and Chairman
LPL Financial

I'm writing this book for a relatively small audience – the 10 to 15 percent of you who are coachable when it comes to your financial future. Unfortunately, most people are so preoccupied with the spending habits they have cultivated throughout their lives, they are not willing to learn. No matter what they might read or hear from me or any other financial advisor, they will probably ignore the message because they would rather risk their financial future than change their habits. There is little I can do for these people.

Occasionally in this book I will use the term "losing decision," and it's important you understand what I am referring to when I do. It's not intended to be harsh or accusatory. Instead, I use the term to differentiate those who are moneyholics and find if difficult to deny themselves of anything, from those who are willing to sacrifice immediate gratification for the promise of a more successful financial future.

So when I talk about a losing strategy, I am not trying to disparage anyone. I realize that not everyone will want to hear my message; I'm okay with that. I also know there are people wealthier than me. My goal is to help these readers recognize and attain their full financial potential so they can be even more efficient and effective and, in turn, help others. After all, isn't it important that we make the most out of what we are given? We can do this by minimizing the myths of Wall Street and financial planning and maximizing the truths of financial success.

My personal dream is to give back to others less fortunate – whether locally, nationally or globally. I want to give generations of people the same opportunities to become successful that I had. I want my legacy to be that I had a positive impact on thousands of people and they, in turn, affected tens of thousands more. For me, that's what being my best means.

I don't know what being your best means to you. For most readers, it probably entails some form of financial success. However, if you spend your days trying to find happiness by spending your wealth on things you really don't need, you will have missed a chance to turn it into opportunities for others.

My task in this book is to help you find contentment and happiness in living a simpler, but more successful financial life. I want to help you better focus on what your purpose in life is, and consider ways you can give to others.

Often, a small but consequential ripple on the ocean can result in huge changes and opportunities for those less fortunate on the other side. I hope to show you how leaving a legacy can have a positive effect for generations to come.

I challenge you to think more deeply about your life and your decisions. Take time to determine what it is you need to comfortably sustain your lifestyle, and then consider anything beyond that as excess wealth. If you can learn to be happy with what you have, be prudent, and avoid buying things you really don't need simply because you can, you can find true contentment by giving a portion of the excess to others.

If everybody was 20 percent more successful and gave half of that back to some worthy cause, we could literally change the world. So much good could be done with the wealth and opportunities it provides. Whatever your cause, financial success will allow you to expand your success to others and help them become successful and perhaps help others. Perhaps more importantly, people 50 or 100 years from now will know you lived and did something to make life and the world better, just by being on the planet.

There is only one "richest person" in the world and even that title changes from time to time. No matter how much we accumulate, there will always be someone with more than us. Winners are happy with what they have, and they don't pursue money and things just for the sake of having more. They also accept the fact that sometimes they may make losing decisions. However, this doesn't make them losers. Unlike losers who tend to avoid decisions and expect someone else to come to their rescue when they make mistakes, winners take responsibility for their mistakes and try to do better.

Those who will read and respond to the concepts in this book are people who want to take responsibility for their financial future by making winning decisions. Chances are, they are already winners. They are probably people who are, or will be successful and have the opportunity to do something meaningful with their wealth. With just a few small changes, you can become one of them. You have the potential of becoming better – a better spouse, parent, community or church member. "Winning decisions" allow people to grow, make changes and become better managers of their financial futures. This book was written to give you some of the tools to help you attain a successful financial future. And, with the help of a competent and caring financial professional, you can. I want you to be a winner! A significant force to those around you. In doing this, we need to harvest your potential by finding your unique financial DNA.

Wayne von Borstel

Wayne von Borstel, CFP®, CLU, ChFC, MSFS
President and Founder
von Borstel & Associates, Inc.

1

Changing Our
Financial Attitude

*"The lack of clear financial direction can leave
anyone susceptible to stress and uncertainty."*
– Wayne von Borstel

Watching TV, you can hardly miss the commercials that portray a microcosm of our evolving culture. A car company shows some wide-eyed people gawking enviously at a young couple driving past in their sleek new sedan. A diet plan features former jocks describing how they recaptured their youthful, athletic bodies while eating pizza, hamburgers and lasagna. A company that buys structured settlements from desperate consumers for cents on the dollar features angry people hanging out of windows, screaming "It's my money and I want it now!"

As a society, we've been conditioned to believe that happiness is the result of driving the right car, choosing the right diet or having more money to spend. Breweries tell us romance is a matter of choosing the right beer. We are deluged with these messages daily and, after a time, we subconsciously begin to believe them. The marketers who promote these fantasies are not content to merely convince us we need what they have to sell, they take it one step further by telling us we can have a carefree, satisfying life by buying their product, and there's no need to wait. We can have it all right now!

Want to drive a car that makes your neighbors jealous? Lease it today with no money down. Want a big house? Take out an interest-only loan with 3% down. Think you deserve a great vacation? Use your credit card to charge it. Virtually anything you think will make you happy is available today and can be paid for later.

A National Spending Addiction

As a society, we have contracted a national illness: moneyholism. We are addicted to spending. The addiction permeates virtually every aspect of our lives as individuals and our society as a whole, yet it is rarely characterized or discussed as a problem. The meager attempts made to address the problem erroneously focus on the symptoms instead of the disease. Giving moneyholics access to credit is like giving alcoholics a glass of wine to pacify their thirst.

As a nation, we have succumbed to the addiction of relentlessly chasing money and spending it. As bad as this compulsion is, a more ominous danger lies in buying into the castle-in-the-sky vision promoted by the Wall Street marketing machine. Like their counterparts working in the automobile, entertainment, clothing, jewelry and other industries, those responsible for pushing products at wirehouses, brokerage firms or insurance companies all have the same assignment: to make their firm's skunks look like cuddly kittens. And financial skunks are the worst of the lot because once you discover you bought one, you can't go back and get a refund or exchange it for something better.

Selling the idea that we can become wealthy by buying something that is likely not in our best interest, financial firms prey on our underlying belief that we need wealth to be happy; we have to buy a financial product that will allow us to beat the market, become wealthy and find bliss. The unspoken, implicit message in all of this is that we cannot be happy with what we already have because if we believed that, there would be no reason to buy what Wall Street is selling.

While behavior modification may help a person recover from a spending addiction, the toxic impact of making poor investment choices based on Wall Street marketing or the advice of media talking heads may be irreversible. It's a skunk that moves in and never leaves.

We Can't All be Above Average

In addition to the unceasing onslaught of financial pornography, another cause of flawed investment decisions is overconfidence. Most people think they are better at almost anything than they really are. Perhaps the most celebrated better-than-average finding is a study conducted by O. Svenson that found 93% of American drivers rated themselves as being better drivers than the median[1]. Of course, it's impossible for 93% of drivers to be better than average, so that means at least 43% of the drivers surveyed viewed themselves as being better drivers than they actually were. It's much the same with investing. Regardless of investment results, most people believe they are smart investors. They explain away poor performance as bad timing or just plain bad luck.

Overconfidence is a symptom displayed by the middle class and wealthy alike. The only difference may be the size of their portfolios and the scope of their investment decisions. Similarly, both are vulnerable to spending addictions that prevent them from reaching their financial goals. People can have a high net worth and still not have assets that generate sufficient income to meet their lifestyle requirements.

Often, those who earn $100,000 a year live hand-to-mouth and have no savings. They may never have learned how to save, or how to deny themselves an extravagance. They may not know how to be content with what they have or know how to invest

---

1 Svenson, O. (1981). Are we less risky and more skillful than our fellow drivers? Acta Psychologic, 47, 143-151.

wisely. Snared in a perpetual financial trap, they are unable to free themselves and move forward.

Conversely, there are people who are worth millions of dollars and have a spending addiction or lack a sound financial plan, or both. Despite their wealth, they need more income to support their lifestyle; they choose to live in bigger houses and buy more expensive toys. These people may be no closer to meeting their long-term financial goals than are the struggling middle-class wage earners.

The lack of clear financial direction can leave anyone susceptible to stress and uncertainty, particularly when a severe market downturn or unexpected event in their life triggers stressful decisions. With no reliable plan, they lose faith in their own judgment. They look for solutions in the advice offered by financial product providers, mass media talking heads or well-intentioned friends. They end up chasing investment returns and taking on more risk. Every morning they go online and sweat the markets. They have no peace, and the outcome is rarely positive.

Chart 1.1 INVESTOR DILEMMA

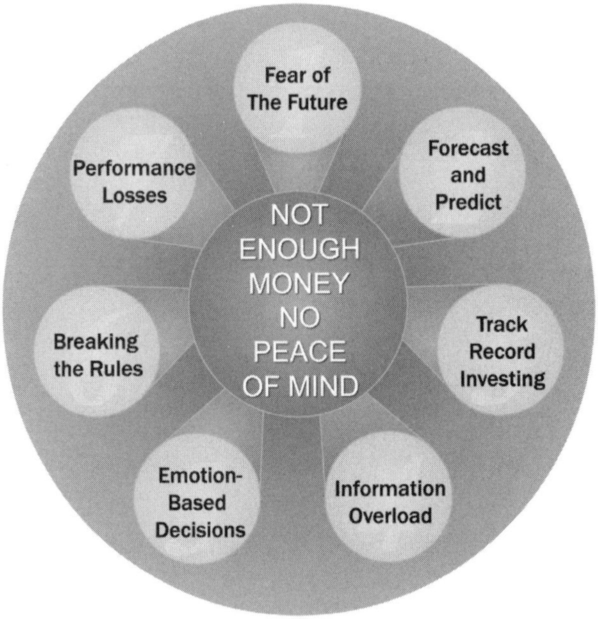

Chart provided by Matson Money

There is an inextricable link between overconfidence, spending addictions, omnipresent financial pornography and the irrational pursuit of unrealistic investment returns.

During the past 27 years, countless people have come into my office and asked how they can earn double-digit portfolio returns every year to support their lifestyle. They never ask how to get their spending habits under control or how to build a financial defense against the inevitable tough times. They don't want to talk about the mundane process of planning and budgeting. They just want the final piece of the financial puzzle so they can maintain their current lifestyle and spending habits. They want to find a magic formula that generates lofty investment returns and never has a down year.

Of course, no such formula exists, any more than the financial analyst on CNN can predict next year's market winners. No advisor can provide the final piece of the financial puzzle without first determining what the total picture looks like. They need to take the time to empty the box, spread out all the pieces, and locate all the corners and edges. And, while the most important piece may be the last one, when starting out they have no idea what piece that is. There's a myth that the final piece lies in getting the highest possible portfolio return; however, putting the puzzle together is all about identifying your goals, and then knowing if you are on track to reach those goals. It's the only way to get to that final, fulfilling piece that completes the puzzle while also helping protect against the unknowns.

Then and Now

People talk about how tough our lives are today, and how it is so much harder financially than it was in years past. They say kids today have no real chance for financial success. Is this accurate?

In talking about changing people's attitudes, I think back to how things were in the late 1940s in suburban Portland, Oregon. The average size of a home was around 850 square feet, and it typically had two bedrooms that, combined, were smaller than the master bedroom of most homes today. There was one bathroom to serve the average family of five to six people; it was nothing like the luxurious bathrooms we have today. Roughly half the homes had a garage because only half of the families owned a car. Instead, people took the bus or walked to work and school. There were no televisions and children were expected to go outside and play for recreation, learning to socialize with other children in the process.

Yet many people believe previous generations had it better than we do, that things are much tougher today. Really? Today, many children are so addicted to television, computer games, cell phones and other electronic gizmos that they cannot tolerate silence. Their attention spans have shrunk to the point they cannot function without constantly being in touch with friends on Facebook or MySpace. Often, they ignore the person they are with while they text yet another person. They want everything television advertising tells them they should have, and they expect their parents to buy it. Kids haven't learned to do without.

As adults, we must set a good example for our kids. We need to stay out of debt, and not spend tomorrow's income on things we really do not need. We do not need to fill up our homes, closets and garages with things that may be fun to have, but are unnecessary and often cause us more concern.

I know people who earn $12,000 a month and have no money. They spend it on things they want or think will make their lives better, but these *things* can't make them happy. Purchasing things we do not need only makes our lives more complicated and difficult. Most of the people in the world have nowhere near as much as we Americans have, yet we feel the need to continuously buy more stuff. Do we really need these things to have good life?

I sincerely believe everyone in our country could live on substantially less than what they currently spend. If we simplify our lives, buying only the things we *really* need, we can be just as happy or happier, and we will vastly improve our chances for financial success.

The 5% Solution

One day a client told me she wanted to liquidate her variable annuity ASAP. When I asked why, she replied, "Suze Orman said variable annuities are just a commission-generating gimmick for advisors and she would not own one under any circumstances."

This client is an educated woman who has built a successful business, earns more than a quarter of a million dollars a year and has a net worth that would allow her to retire comfortably tomorrow, if she so desired. She is nobody's fool. Yet, a two-minute TV segment prompted her to make a financial decision with little factual basis. That's the influence the mass media has on our everyday lives.

Obviously, any financial product can be detrimental if used incorrectly or in the wrong circumstances. The reality is, there are no innately good or bad investment products; instead, there are appropriate and inappropriate applications.

For years I have taught financial education classes. It would be presumptuous of me to think that every topic applies to everyone in the class. However, I know that what I say at any given moment will be critical information for a small percentage of those in attendance. What I say 10 minutes later will be critical for others. This is true for any financial concept or idea put forth in a lecture, discussion or book. Not everything pertains to everyone, but what does is essential.

Unfortunately, once a personality has been crowned a financial "guru" by the media, or has been identified by the general public as such, their words can carry unwarranted influence. However, when they make a pronouncement on TV about an investment product or strategy, their assessment likely applies to no more than 5% to 10% of their audience. They are talking to millions of people via the airwaves, and they have no idea who is listening nor do they have any knowledge of each listener's personal circumstances. Everyone's investment requirements and ultimate goals are different. Everyone has a unique puzzle, and chances are what they say applies to 10% or fewer of the listeners.

While most of the information in this book is vital, you may find some of it inessential but worth reviewing. Although a particular subject may not directly apply to your circumstances, it may someday. Even if it never does, the better overall knowledge and understanding you gain, the better your thought process will be. Knowledge will help you make better decisions as you transition through the stages of your financial life. This book does not attempt to provide the final piece of anyone's puzzle. However, it can provide a roadmap to help you find the final piece, and enable you recognize it when you see it.

Helping successful people invest successfully is as much a game of influencing people's habits as it is of controlling investments. Each puzzle must be a sufficiently appealing picture and be put together correctly so its owner will have trust and confidence in good and bad times alike. Much of what a dedicated advisor does is to help people have peace of mind when storms come. And the storms will come. While some professionals in the industry try to predict what's ahead, no one knows when bad times will occur, only that they will. Whatever is going to affect us tomorrow is unknown today. Our only defense is to have a sound plan, be prudent and realistic, control what we can, and stay on track.

> *Our ultimate goal is to achieve peace of mind.*
> *This can be done by investing in a sound and*
> *well-thought-through financial plan.*

Caring About Clients

As a naïve young fellow who left the family farm for a career in financial services, there was much to learn. It soon became apparent that more money could be made by telling people what they wanted to hear, instead of what they needed to hear. By doing this I would have more clients, although not the caliber and quality of clients I wanted. Instead, I made the decision to care more about providing sound financial advice. I wanted to be more concerned about having a positive impact on the lives of my clients than about how much money was coming in the door. Ultimately, this proved to be more rewarding in a variety of ways. The opportunity to have a positive impact on so many lives over the years has been more satisfying than any amount of money I could have earned.

Of course, as a result of *really* caring about my clients I've had to extend myself, investing time others may have viewed as unwarranted. Instead of golfing, fishing or traveling, I chose to help change peoples' lives ... to be significant. Putting one's personal and professional pride on the line each day is the ultimate test of an advisor's commitment. My clients hear the truth, something few financial professionals are willing to risk telling them. They deserve to hear it because they can make better decisions knowing the truth than not. Yes, some will become frustrated and leave when they are told something they don't want to hear, but even so, they are better off having that seed of truth planted in their minds.

Because my clients are a priority, I'm often accused of being a workaholic, and perhaps that's true. On the other hand, my marriage to an incredible woman who has always supported me and understands my goals more than compensates for those sacrifices. Our two children are now doctors and dedicated Christians who, because they have come to understand the importance of caring more about others than themselves, are more likely to excel as professionals. They understand what that difference means to their patients.

As a financial professional, it's impossible to predict how the markets will perform next year and equally difficult to imagine what the financial world will be like in 200 years, but I believe the core truths will still be true and relevant. When it comes to investing, being systematic, unemotional and diversified can help solve many of the financial problems we face. My hope and belief is that the financial wisdom and the core truths I espoused all these years will have a positive effect on the future generations of my clients a century or two from now.

◆◆◆

2

Financial Myths

*"Your best defense against myths is
factually accurate knowledge."*
– Wayne von Borstel

U nfortunately, much of the information re-
lating to money that permeates our thinking as individuals and as a society is based
on myths. This misleading information has no factual basis and can actually prevent us from achieving our financial objectives.

It's important that we become more aware of these
financial myths, as so many of them have become
entrenched in our collective mindset. Very rarely do
people challenge their veracity. Instead they are reinforced daily by a Wall Street marketing machine
and a compliant media that largely depends on Wall
Street advertising dollars to remain in business.

The greatest challenge we face in our financial pur-
suits is to dispel these myths and disregard the marketing foolishness that distorts rational thoughts and
inhibits sound decisions. Pursuing financial success

while pitted against these ill-conceived notions is the toughest, most problematic game we will ever play. You might compare it to playing in the Super Bowl. The game is four quarters long and consists of many individual plays that determine whether a team wins or loses. Similarly, winning our financial future means staying in the game and competing for the full four quarters. If we are armed with factual knowledge, it will give us the confidence we need to ignore the noise of the crowd. We then have a better chance of winning, that is, achieving financial independence and a satisfying, self-reliant life.

Much of the crowd noise we must ignore is in the form of financial myths that many people commonly accept as fact. The following are some of the more common myths.

Myth #1
Planning Stops When You Reach Retirement

People often believe that once they reach retirement they can coast because the game is over. This myth reminds me of a football team that's ahead at halftime and decides not to come out to play the second half. Retirement is merely another event on our life's financial journey. It is not the end of the game. Instead, the planning process will remain significant throughout our lives, right up to the final whistle.

Giving up on planning once we retire allows the heavyweight players, such as taxation and inflation, to knock us out of the game during the second half. These players never quit. Regardless of how far ahead we are at retirement, if we don't come out and play hard in the second half, we are going to lose the game.

Myth #2
My Advisor Can Tell Me What the Markets Will Do

The world's smartest financial advisor can't tell you what the markets will do tomorrow, next week or next month. No one can. No one is privy to that information. The myth that an advisor, broker or investment analyst can accurately foretell what the markets will do is based on the human need to have answers to every question. People so desperately want to know what will happen next, they cling to the notion that there must be someone who can tell them.

If you go to the horse races, you will see people selling "tout sheets" for five or ten dollars that predict the day's winners. Why would someone who supposedly has that information stand out in the hot sun selling it for a few dollars when, instead, they could simply bet on the horses they say will win and celebrate their own fortune? It makes no sense, yet gamblers gobble up tout sheets and bet their money on the predictions.

If anyone truly knew what tomorrow's market was going to do, why would they waste their time telling others about it for a meager television appearance fee when they could use the information to get rich?

The counterpoint to this myth is that asking what the markets will do tomorrow is the wrong question. If you ask your advisor and the answer you get proves to be correct, it isn't because he or she knew something nobody else knew; it's because your advisor guessed and got lucky. It's time to discard the myth that an oracle exists that can show you the shortcut to prosperity. Your financial success is based on how much you save and your ability to develop and maintain prudent, systematic habits. It will not be the result of a dartboard guess or an enchanted investment. Good planning and a systematic process drive financial success, not jumping off a cliff with the rest of the lemmings while chasing the latest *hot dot*.

Myth #3
My Advisor Knows Which Stocks To Buy

Countless times I've spent the better part of an hour trying to convince someone that no one can correctly predict what stock or fund will perform best tomorrow or next year. Finally convinced, he or she will agree that there is no crystal ball for the markets, yet in the next sentence will ask me to pick a stock for them.

There is something ingrained in us that makes us want to believe there is someone who can predict what is going to happen, despite all evidence to the contrary. Innumerable studies have concluded that speculation or trying to time the market does not work over the long haul, yet people remain obsessed with knowing what the future holds.

It's difficult for advisors to get past this obstacle and arrive at a point in their careers that I reached many years ago – the ability to be completely candid with their clients. Some professionals in our industry never get there, because they are often consumed with moving product and making commissions. They fear that if they tell clients they don't know something, the clients will have no reason to buy from them. However, choosing stocks so clients can beat the market is not the preeminent value a competent advisor offers. The chart below (2.1) illustrates how little influence market timing, stock selection and other factors play in helping you reach your financial goals. Instead, proper asset allocation can help provide you with confidence, financial stability and independence.

Chart 2.1 DETERMINANTS OF PORTFOLIO PERFORMANCE

1.8% Market Timing

2.1% Other Factors

4.6% Stock Selection

91.5% Asset Allocation

Market Timing
Other Factors
Stock Selection
Asset Allocation

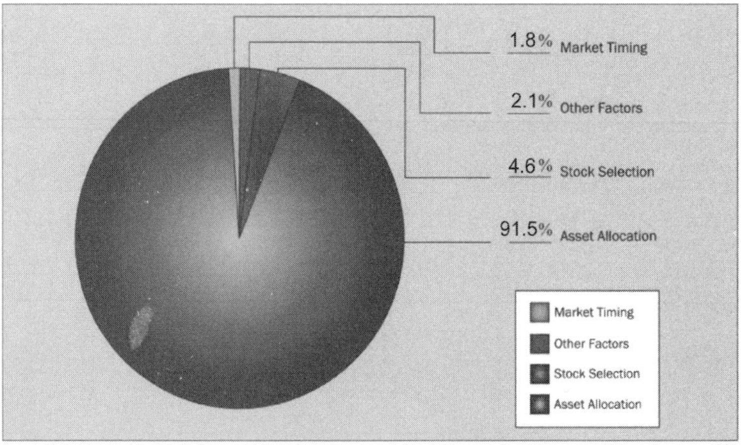

Source: "Determinants of Portfolio Performance," *Financial Analysts Journal*, Gary P. Brinson, L. Randolf Hood, and Gilbert L. Beebower, 1986. "Revisiting Determinants of Portfolio Performance: An Update," Brinson, Singer, Beebower, 1991.

Myth #4
My Broker Has My Best Interest at Heart

Your broker may be a very nice person and say all the right things, but what he or she recommends may or may not be the best fit for your needs. Some brokers can't earn their bonuses unless they sell a certain amount of product. Their paychecks may be contingent upon the type and amount of products they are required to sell – products their company manufactures or makes markets in. So, whether advising a 30 or an 80-year-old client, they disregard the client's individual needs, giving recommendations from the same list of proprietary investments. In addition, huge trading costs can accompany each transaction. (See Chart 2.2)

While this may work for your broker, it's not in your best interest. Instead, it's best to talk to someone who is knowledgeable and has no bias. That is, they have no vested interest in recommending one investment over another based on compensation. Common sense tells us someone with a vested interest is not going to be truly objective.

Chart 2.2 THE COSTS OF TRADING

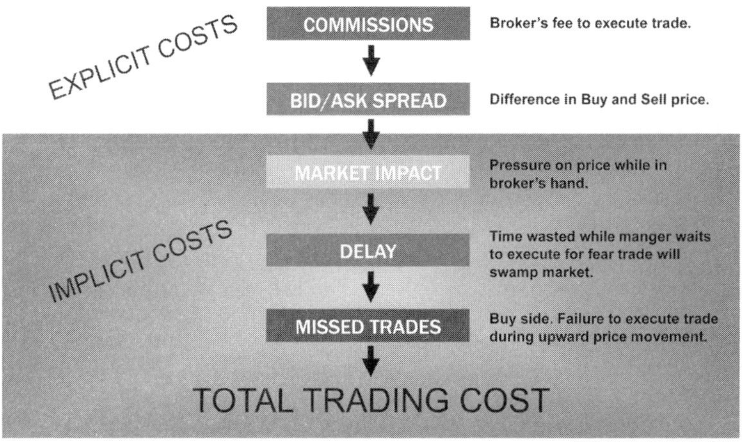

Chart provided by Matson Money

Myth #5
Individual Stocks are the Best Investment

It's surprising how many people embrace this myth. They have been convinced by Wall Street marketing and the media that owning individual equities will produce better results than investment accounts, managed accounts, ETFs or annuities with the promise of cash flow.

Granted, if an individual has sufficient wealth to create a huge portfolio with hundreds of stocks and is able to manage it systematically and unemotionally, he or she may do very well. Perhaps one person in 10,000 has that kind of wealth, and of those maybe one in 1,000 has the financial expertise to manage his or her portfolio proficiently.

The main reason the individual stock myth continues to thrive is that Wall Street makes a lot of money when retail investors buy and sell individual stocks. Then too, people like to trade stocks. It's in their nature to gamble. They like the challenge and the action. Often they're willing to risk their future doing it.

Unfortunately, few investors have the affluence to construct a truly diversified portfolio. It's something that can't be accomplished with 25 or 50 stocks. Instead, the tendency is to become overweighted in a single stock that does really well. Ultimately, the investor will hold on to the stock too long, trying to avoid paying a capital gains tax on the profits. The overweighting also creates heightened exposure as a result of reduced diversification in the portfolio.

It's not uncommon for people to have a portfolio with 30%
or more of it in a single stock. Typically, they've done so
well with that stock they can't afford to sell it and pay the
taxes. Eventually, the stock becomes a dog.

Think about the stocks of the most successful companies just a decade ago. Many high-flyers during the 1990s sank like a rock during the first decade of the new millennium. See examples on the next page (Chart 2.3).

Yes, even the biggest, most successful companies can eventually level off or sink altogether. They grow too large, become ineffective, and lose leadership or market share to better technology. Their stocks react accordingly. Few of today's great companies will still be great 10 or 15 years from now. The dangers associated with owning individual stocks makes the strategy unwise for all but the very wealthy, and not many of them.

Chart 2.3 STOCK COMPARISONS FROM 1990s AND 2000s

STOCK	1990s Results	2000s Results
Dell	+89,000%	-73%
Microsoft	+9,500%	-48%
Sun Micro	+7,000%	-94%
Intel	+3,700%	-53%
Home Depot	+3,700%	-58%
Amgen	+5,800%	-08%

USA Today, 12/17/2009. Past performance is no guarantee of future results.

NOTE: Stock investing involves risk, including loss of principal. There is no guarantee that a diversified portfolio will enhance overall returns or outperform a non-diversified portfolio. Diversification does not protect against market risk.

Myth #6
Fallacy of the Separately Managed Account

Many people believe driving a fancier car will make them happier than driving a cheaper model. If they have a larger amount of money, they feel obliged to drive a Mercedes rather than a Chevrolet. Similarly, some people believe they need a separately managed account.[1] Having a managed account is like having a Rolls Royce to prove you are successful. It helps people feel good and Wall Street perpetuates the myth that wealthier investors do better if they have one. It's the Rolls Royce of investing.

Managed accounts have advantages and disadvantages, but they are no panacea for the wealthy. And, purchasing a managed account based on previous performance is downright silly.

---

1 The term Separately Managed Account (SMA) is used by the brokerage industry whereby an account is managed by portfolio management resources within the firm, or more commonly, by an outside money management firm along with an administrator. In this context, an SMA can be thought of as an investment vehicle similar to a mutual fund where a fee is paid to the money manager for its services managing the customer's investment. The important difference is that a mutual fund investor owns shares of a company that in turn owns other investments, whereas SMA investors own the invested assets directly in their own name.

Very few managed accounts are based on academic principles or prudent portfolio practices. Most are based on the myth that their manager is a financial wizard or has some extraordinary talent for beating the market. A better criterion would be to have a managed account designed to your specific needs and risk tolerance.

Myth #7
The Best Investment is...

This myth would probably have died long ago were it not for the inexhaustible efforts of Wall Street's marketing machine. Understand this: There is no *best* investment. Every legitimate investment product has its place.

I have yet to find an investor brought to financial ruin because they bought the wrong investment product. On the other hand, I know far too many people who have experienced financial ruin because they have no financial plan or have one that is inferior. Deep financial trouble is almost always caused by the lack of solid planning, the inability to save, or a spending addiction. Aside from fraudulent financial schemes, financial woes are almost never the result of choosing inappropriate investment products.

Chart 2.4 THE RISK OF CHANGING INVESTMENT STRATEGIES

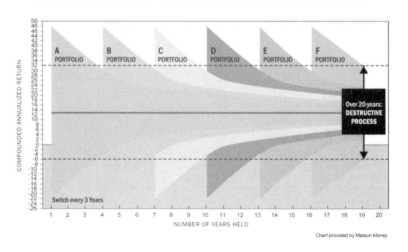

Chart provided by Matson Money

18

People get into trouble quickly when they lack a process that is systematic, unemotional and diversified. Often they end up chasing investment returns, looking for that perfect product that doesn't exist. They leapfrog from one strategy to another, never settling on an appropriate and consistent long-term strategy, and never achieving the results they hoped for.

Myth #8
I Can Beat the Market

No one comes back from Las Vegas and admits losing his shirt. With all those winners, it's amazing that Las Vegas survives, let alone thrives. Similarly, no one wants to admit to investment losses. Instead, everyone thinks they can beat the markets. However, if they could wouldn't they all be billionaires? But they're not.

When people want to believe something is true, they usually can find justification for doing so. Some get up every day convinced they will weigh a pound less tomorrow. They rationalize that somehow the weight will fall off. However, if they don't change their diets and exercise habits, they are only fooling themselves. There are lots of golfers who think buying the newest equipment will improve their game. Constantly changing equipment misses the point, however. Improvement typically requires professional help and a consistent approach. The same applies to investing.

Those who try to beat the market by continuously changing their investment strategy generally end up back where they started ... or worse. Missing just 10 of the best days in a decade can reduce portfolio returns by roughly 37%, as evidenced by Chart 2.5 on page 20.

People may think they are better at investing than they are. However, you can't outwit the stock market, and certainly not on a consistent basis.

Chart 2.5 WHY MARKET TIMING DOESN'T WORK

January 1, 1996 – December 31, 2006

2,520 Trading Days

	Return of S&P 500 Index	Growth of $10,000 Investment *
Fully Invested	8.33%	$22,252
Missed 10 best days	3.32%	$13,864
Missed 20 best days	-0.46%	$9,548
Missed 30 best days	-3.71%	$6,649
Missed 40 best days	-6.42%	$5,148
Missed 60 best days	-10.98%	$3,125

*Based on Initial Invesment of $10,000   Chart provided by Matson Money
Indexes, such as the S&P 500, cannot be bought into directly.

Myth #9
Greater Risk Generates Greater Returns

Someone may have told you that if you want better returns, you must take more risk. That's bunk. Taking more risk may or may not produce better returns; it definitely produces more risk. Non-prudent risk creates more excitement – it's like financial bungee jumping. However, a passive portfolio is more likely to deliver better results. It's like the difference between bungee jumping and taking a peaceful stroll through the woods.

Added portfolio risk may generate enhanced returns, but it may also generate greater losses. It's difficult to overcome large portfolio losses, and suffering large losses often tempts investors to take even greater risks, trying to recoup those losses.

Most investors equate risk with equities. But risk exists in virtually every investment product. It also resides in events and elements related to investment products, including mismanaged companies, broken promises, changing markets and inflation. Not long ago, inflation was the biggest risk faced by investors. One day it will be again. Inflation is the silent assassin of portfolio growth. Even if you bury your money in the ground, it's not safe from inflation.

While there is no way to completely eliminate risk, a well-constructed portfolio may mitigate risks of all types.

Myth #10
I Can't Afford to Save

Years ago I worked with young couples who would say they couldn't afford to put $300 a month into a college savings plan for their children. However, when I drove past their houses I would see new SUVs in their driveways. I'm sure they cost at least $500 a month.

People can always find money for the things they want badly enough, yet can't seem to find money for savings or an emergency fund. Not being able to save is a myth based on lack of motivation.

Myth #11
There's Never a Good Time to Save

Over the past three decades, I've probably heard every excuse known to man as to why people can't save. Those in their 20s are too young to listen; in their 30s, it costs too much to raise children so they'll have to wait; in their 40s, they can't believe how expensive it is educate their teenagers; and in their 50s, they are tired and just want to survive until retirement ... besides, it's too late, isn't it?

Those same people wake up in their 60s and ask, "Why didn't someone help me save money for retirement when I was younger?" The myth is, there's never a good time to start. The reality is, there is no shortage of excuses to rationalize not saving. The truth is, there will never be a better day to start saving than today. You will never have as much time to save again.

Myth #12
I Can Live On Half of What I Do Now When I Retire

Many people believe that once they retire, they can live comfortably on a fraction of their current income. If you buy into this myth, practice it for a year and see if you can do it.

Of course, rarely does anyone put this suggestion into practice. The reality is, almost no one can do it this year or when they retire. The older we get, the more we care about money. Our dignity over the long term depends on having enough money to pay for our own groceries, utilities, healthcare and the like. At age 102, my grandmother cared more about being able to write checks and preserve her dignity than she did at age 65.

People fool themselves about how much money they will need after retirement. However, whatever they spend today, they will more than likely want to spend the same amount once they retire. Most have developed spending habits they are comfortable with, and they won't want to change them.

Myth #13
Retirement Calls for a More
Conservative Investment Strategy

Investing is a lifetime activity. Retirement is a blip on that continuum. Changing risk parameters at retirement makes no sense. Instead, retirees should be in a financial position where there is no need to change investment strategies. Those who achieve the four principles listed in the Core Truths section (Chapter Three) have no need to make dramatic shifts at retirement.

The myth of "shifting gears" at retirement is actively perpetuated by the financial services industry, in particular by Wall Street. The brokers who sold you product during the past 30 or 40 years never helped you create a solid plan. They didn't care whether you were successful in attaining your goals, as long as you kept buying what they were selling. Now that you are approaching retirement, they want to talk to you about "red zone" investing, a term some brokerage firms use when referring to the five years before and after retirement. All of a sudden they want to help you get serious about your goals? What a joke.

Investing to reach financial success is a lifetime process.

Whatever age you begin, you need to match your investment strategy with an appropriate and prudent risk tolerance. That's something you do for a lifetime, not something to start thinking about a few years before you retire. The problem is, some professionals in our industry don't spend much time matching investors to their specific risk tolerance. Two different people in virtually identical financial situations may need different risk tolerance strategies because they have dissimilar financial DNAs, and they react differently to the markets.

Those who change their risk tolerance strategies every few years are unlikely to ever reach financial success. They will have the same potential for failure 20 years from now as they do today. The risk of failure is significantly heightened by frequent shifts in investment philosophy. Instead, it's important to choose a strategy with an appropriate risk tolerance and stay true to it. (See Chart 2.4, page 18)

Myth #14
I Know My Risk Tolerance

The financial services industry has designations for levels of risk tolerance – conservative, moderately aggressive and aggressive. Analysts, advisors and investors alike use these terms in an effort to describe their capacity for portfolio risk. While the same term often means different things to different people, no one challenges the definitions.

It's convenient and comforting to assign terminology to various investment styles. The financial industry reinforces this practice. Investment managers ostensibly match client portfolios with an investment style that, supposedly, matches the client's comfort level.

Here's where the myth comes in: Typically, the manager and the clients only have a vague notion of what the terminology they are using means, or even if they are speaking the same language. Two people can use the same term, such as "moderate," and mean very different levels of risk. Where did these terms come from? Who bothers to assess what they mean? No one really knows. They're conversational conveniences that have no relation to standard deviation, nor are they a reliable measure of portfolio risk.

An experience I had with a lady in her 80s is a good example of how this myth can have unintended and potentially toxic effects. She asked me to take over management of her portfolio after her long-time advisor died. She repeatedly stressed that she didn't want me to change anything; but, instead, to maintain the staunchly conservative investment strategy her deceased advisor had created. Her primary concern was the safety of her principal and a guaranteed income.

I assumed there wasn't much I could do for this elderly woman until I reviewed her portfolio. I was astonished to find more than 90% of her holdings were in equities! She assured me she and her former advisor had many conversations and always agreed to an ultra-conservative risk tolerance. How could an advisor translate that message into a heavy weighting in equities? While they both used the same terminology when they spoke, obviously they had totally different interpretations.

An academic approach that measures the potential risk can be assigned to any portfolio. If you can't accurately determine the potential loss for your portfolio in any given year, you and your advisor are not speaking the same language, and that's a dangerous practice.

Myth #15
I Can't Have Lazy Dollars in My Portfolio

Some people are averse to having an emergency fund that's not earning anything, so they never create one. What they fail to understand is that over the long term, having an emergency fund they can tap into any time they *really need it* means their other dollars can work harder, seek better growth and be more tax advantaged. However, if they lack an emergency fund, their portfolio must have greater liquidity, ensuring funds are available for emergencies. That translates into less flexibility in growth strategies, tax planning and other investment considerations.

Keep in mind that the fund must be maintained for emergencies only, not as a spending addiction facilitator. This way, should something unforeseen occur, portfolio assets won't have to be liquidated at a disadvantageous time or suffer a withdrawal penalty. The emergency fund is like oil for the portfolio engine, helping it run longer and more smoothly. The cost of the oil is a minor consideration against a potential engine blowup. Similarly, liquidity is crucial to a successful financial plan. The relatively few lazy dollars that comprise an emergency fund serve as vital insurance for your portfolio.

Myth #16
I Am My Own Financial Coach

Even the best players in what may be the most difficult individual sport, golf, all have a coach. These champions have been playing golf since childhood and understand every nuance of the game, yet they don't trust their own instincts to avoid or correct problems that inevitably arise. Instead, they rely on their coaches to see what they can't see. The greatest athletes in virtually every sport trust their coaches to help them maximize their talents, control their emotions and win consistently. They would never think of training or competing without having a professional coach guide them.

However, people take on one of the most complicated and mentally challenging games in the world — financial planning, and they expect to beat the markets without professional coaching. Is it any wonder so many fail? The wealthy are not exempt. They make mistakes as well. The difference is, they can make errors and still remain wealthy. Most people can't. Regardless of how much or how little money someone has, they need a coach to oversee their choices and be there when they encounter situations that call for financial savvy and experience. A financial coach can be their advocate, help them get through bad days without making hasty or emotionally charged decisions, and help them see outside the box when necessary.

Myth #17
Financial Success Equates With
How Much Money You Make

This is a monster of a myth and insidious because so many people accept it as gospel. Here's the reality: Financial success has *zero* correlation to how much money you make; it has a 100% correlation to how you *plan* and how much you *save*.

When I was young and working with people who made modest incomes, it was much easier to motivate them to plan and save because they recognized if they didn't do the right things, they would be in financial trouble. On the other hand, people who make a great deal of money are frequently so addicted to having and spending money that they can't see the inherent danger in not planning and saving. Adept at making money, they see wealth as a given, a backyard tree that eternally blossoms with a fruit called money. Making money comes so easy to them that they feel no urgency to save.

I sometimes think there is a reverse correlation between the amount of money someone makes and their financial success and happiness. Many of the wealthy believe nothing bad can happen to them, that they are immune to the obstacles and uncertainty life throws at everyone else. Because life is so easy for them, they forget they need to come out on the field and play the game.

On the other hand, people struggling with finances know bad things can and do happen. They feel more of an urgency to prepare for these situations. They understand the necessity of playing the game.

Myth #18
It's Different This Time

Whenever something happens in the markets that people perceive as "out of the ordinary," you will hear this myth. The media immediately picks up the myth and reinforces it by having the talking head tell us why (they think) it is different this time and the worse things get, they more they reiterate.

It may well be *somewhat* different every time, just as each hurricane season is somewhat different than the others. But when the market is in freefall, no one knows whether it will continue down or bounce back up tomorrow, next week or next month. No one knows if the next 20% movement will be up or down. The one thing we do know is that, over the long term, the market will go up. The history of the market tells us that.

The free markets work because they go wherever there is profit, whether in China, Japan, South America, India or the USA. I hope it is in the USA; but if not, there still will be profits somewhere and free markets will be at work. There are more people with access to free markets today than ever before in history. Bad things will continue to happen. There will always be natural disasters, wars and crazy people creating havoc, and those events will affect the markets in the short term. But as long as free markets exist, there will continue to be profits and growth somewhere.

So, no matter what the talking heads are saying about it being "different this time," it's not all *that* different.

Myth #19
My Estate Plan is Complete

After reviewing some 600 estate plans over the past three decades, I have yet to see an estate plan that is complete or without omissions. In some cases, the owner's net worth was in the tens-of-millions of dollars, yet it made no difference when it came to accurateness. While most of these people thought their plans reflected their precise wishes, not one did. In every instance, something had to be revised or changed, often several things ... and sometimes, big things.

How do you know if your estate plan is good? What is good? Good is what you know for certain after a discovery process, uncovering information about the potential errors, inaccuracies and unintended consequences. It's amazing how many times something occurs in a plan that inadvertently causes battles between family members after the owner is deceased. Wealthy people often comment that the division of their estate won't be a problem because their heirs "will have more than I had. They can figure it out after I'm gone."

This kind of thinking is common among people who own businesses, farms or real estate. Their viewpoint is understandable; there should be plenty for everyone. No one wants the wealth they leave to cause their grandchildren to hate each other, but it happens far more often than you might think.

The myth is that estate plans are about money. They are not. Estate plans are about people.

Myth #20
Life Insurance is a Fool's Game

When listening to their parents, some people absorbed the myth that life insurance is money poorly spent. Malcolm Forbes, the flamboyant billionaire who founded *Forbes Magazine*, evidently disagreed. Known for his financial savvy, Forbes once responded to a question as to why he reportedly owned a $40 million insurance policy: "Because no one will sell me $60 million!"

Forbes spent money lavishly, but when it came to his estate plan he was no fool. He knew that every dollar in his estate would only be worth 50 cents to his son unless it was free from taxation, which the life insurance proceeds were. So, although life insurance can be foolish if inappropriately placed, it can also be a sage financial choice.

Is permanent life insurance (typically a whole life policy) wrong for someone who can't afford it? Yes. Similarly, if someone needs long-term life insurance coverage and instead rents it using term insurance, that's a misapplication as well. Like any financial product, life insurance can be good or bad, depending on the circumstances. The mistake people make is letting the myth drive their decision without knowing the relevant facts.

Myth #21
COBRA Insurance Gives Me 18 Months of
Breathing Room

COBRA insurance allows certain former employees, retirees, spouses and dependent children the right to temporary continuation of health coverage at group rates. It can be a financial band-aid for many, but it can be a disaster in disguise for those who retire prior to age 65 believing they have 18 months on COBRA to figure things out.

The potential for calamity, and I have seen this happen many times, lies in a person suffering a serious illness or disabling event during that 18-month period. If a heart attack or life-threatening illness renders the person uninsurable, they are in deep financial trouble the day their COBRA coverage expires. It's a worst-case situation because that is precisely when they will need coverage the most.

Those using COBRA must adopt a sense of urgency in securing permanent health coverage. The older a person is, the more pressing the issue.[2]

Myth #22
My Kids Will Have More Than I Did

As a society, we assume it's our children's birthright to have more than we do. It's not. It's important to abandon this myth for several reasons: 1) economically, it's probably not true, and 2) mathematically, it's probably not feasible. Perhaps even more importantly, it's a dangerous presumption because children expect it to happen without effort, promoting an attitude of entitlement.

In the past, people worked for the privilege of a better life. Today, many erroneously believe it will happen automatically because they live in America. Many parents believe that somehow, per-

2 You should talk with a local health care expert who is familiar with the laws in your state that affect your ability to continue health coverage after retirement and before Medicare comes into effect.

haps by osmosis, their children will become wealthy, successful, and know how to manage and save money. Yet they fail to teach their children how to achieve any of these things.

The only way the next generation will have more than this one is if they are smarter, start earlier and work harder than their parents. Otherwise, there is a big chance they'll have less, instead of more.

Myth #23
The New (House, Car, Boat) Will Bring Me Happiness

Advertisers spend billions to convince us we will be happy if we buy their products. The subliminal message is: the more you have, the happier you will be.

Meanwhile, roughly three million Americans who chased happiness filed for bankruptcy during 2009 and 2010.[3]

In my experience of helping people to try to overcome their spending addictions, two irrefutable lessons emerge:

The more things you buy, the more debt you take on, the more complicated your life becomes and the less happy you are.

The simpler your life, the fewer possessions you feel compelled to own, the less stress you will have … and more money.

Possessions cost money. They require maintenance, which costs more money. They break down, costing even more money. They give us grief, often are used only occasionally, and after a short time we grow tired or bored with them and want something new to rekindle our excitement. The more addicted we are to things, the unhappier we are likely to be.

Myth #24
I'm Entitled to a Satisfying Life

One of saddest myths is that people believe they are entitled

3 www.uscourts.gov/uscourts/Statistics/BankruptcyStatistics

to a life of ease and luxury. While you won't hear people say it in so many words, their attitude is unmistakable. They treat themselves to credit card-financed vacations they can't afford because they "deserve some time off." They buy luxury items they don't need and often can't pay for, while rationalizing their spending with, "I'm worth it."

How many commercials have you seen that include the lines, "You deserve," or "You're worth it?" Unfortunately, our government contributes to the myth with an increase of entitlement programs that foster irresponsibility as much as they help those truly in need.

We are not owed anything in life, save for the rights guaranteed by our Constitution. God never promised we could all be millionaires with timeshares in Monaco and Hawaii. There's nothing wrong with aspiring to acquire the nicer things in life. However, when a citizenry starts to believe they are owed those luxuries, we are in trouble. We cannot spend our way to a good life. If we are decent people and are nice to others, we will probably have a satisfying life. If we believe we are owed something because life has not been fair to us or we have suffered some bad luck, we buy into the myth and are certain to suffer disillusionment.

Conclusion

These are the most common myths that confuse people and often cause them to make poor financial decisions. Most of them are perpetuated by those who stand to benefit most from their continuation – namely financial product marketers and an accommodating media. Your best defense against these myths is factually accurate knowledge. In the next chapter, you will learn the Core Truths.

◆◆◆

3

Core Truths

*"You must be able to recognize misguided advice
or outright propaganda when you hear it
and have the confidence to ignore it."*

– Wayne von Borstel

Like your fingerprints and genetic code, you have
your own individual financial DNA. Your financial
personality is the result of a combination of elements, including what you learned as a child from
watching your parents, what you have gleaned as
an adult from friends and associates, and the popu-
lar *financial myths* perpetuated by the media and the
omnipresent marketing machines of Wall Street. The
concepts, beliefs and concerns you hold as truths today are the result of a lifetime of impressions and
messages, many of which likely took up residence
without your knowledge, by osmosis if you will.

In order to reach financial independence, you must
be able to separate misinformation from reality. The
media and the product sellers who support it try to
sell you misinformation or financial "truths" that

have no basis. Well-intentioned friends and associates offer advice but their financial DNA is not the same as yours. You must be able to recognize misguided advice or outright propaganda when you hear it and have the confidence to ignore it. That confidence comes from having a sound financial plan based on *core truths*. These principles will help you make calm, reasoned decisions, regardless of unforeseen events or turmoil that may occur. No matter what happens tomorrow or next year, you must replace financial myths with core truths or you will find it more difficult to become financially successful.

Following are some of the core truths I have learned during my life. I have taught them to people for nearly three decades to help them ignore the noise of the crowd, cultivate a healthy financial DNA, and move confidently toward financial independence and serenity.

Core Truth #1
Investing Should be Systematic, Unemotional and Diversified

This is vital! You must have a systematic investment strategy that avoids portfolio overlap and style drift, and is allocated based on academic asset classes that will allow you to remain calm during economic storms. Being confident in your long-term strategy and shielding yourself against portfolio overweighting will allow you to control what can be controlled.

In contrast, the concept of active management delivering superior investment results can easily be refuted by historical data. The relentless marketing efforts of Wall Street, buttressed by a compliant media, conspires to keep investors emotionally engaged, ceaselessly trading and chasing returns. This frenzy leads to stressful and reactive decision-making that often causes investors to take unnecessary risks as they try to recoup previous losses.

Core Truth #2
"Peace of Mind" Should be Your Goal

While most people consider retirement to be a goal, it shouldn't be. Instead, your goal should be to achieve financial independence. With proper planning, retirement can become a minor event, or a non-event – just one more occurrence in the continuum of life. There is an untold number of small decisions to be made along that continuum. Those decisions will help determine what you will have later in life in terms of wealth, happiness and lifestyle freedom.

Core Truth #3
Your Financial DNA is Unique

As previously mentioned, everyone has his or her own individual financial fingerprint and it's important to know what your financial DNA is. The lifestyle and plan that works for your friend or neighbor may not be right for you.

Consider the couple that lives at 123 Main Street. They own a home with no mortgage. They live simply and do not travel much. They eat at home, volunteer at the community library, and enjoy reading, gardening and taking long walks together. They live on $2,000 a month and usually have money left over.

Next door to them lives a couple who belongs to the country club, dines out regularly, takes cruises and collects fine wines. They drive a new luxury car and have season tickets to the opera. Their $12,000 a month income barely covers their expenses, and they never have money left over.

From the outside, both of their homes look a lot alike, except for the toys in the garage and driveway. But there is a vast difference in their lifestyles, needs and the financial DNAs of these two couples. Similarly, your financial DNA differs from well-meaning neighbors, friends or colleagues who so freely give you misleading advice.

Core Truth #4
Planning Is a Process, Not an Event

Planning is an ongoing process that responds to the inevitable changes life throws at us. It is not something done once and disregarded. Planning should be done as early as possible and reinforced regularly so that it becomes a habit. It then becomes easier to do, than not.

While a rigorous planning process is indispensable for later life success, few people invest adequate time, if any, developing a financial roadmap. Most spend more time planning their summer vacation than they do planning their financial future. They believe there will always be time to start tomorrow, while each year the hill leading to financial independence gets steeper and steeper. The time to start planning is NOW!

Core Truth #5
Everyone Needs a Coach

For most people, achieving financial success is the most complex and difficult task of a lifetime. No matter how much they know, they are almost certain to do better with the help of an experienced financial coach.

Some people think of a financial coach as a sort of crisis counselor, not unlike the surgeon who saves them after a heart attack. Once the crisis has passed, they go back to their normal habits, hopeful it was a one-time event.

Similarly, people facing a financial crisis may seek a coach, hoping for a quick diagnosis and treatment so they can get back to their customary spending activities. For those lacking a solid plan, financial crises are rarely a singular event but rather a series of recurring events. Like a chronic illness, remedial treatment calls for continued behavior modification.

Core Truth #6
Start Saving Now, However Small

If you are not already saving, start now! For many people, the most difficult aspect of saving is getting started. That's probably not news to most people. However, what is shocking is that in the richest country in the history of the world, 76% of retirees have less than $50,000 in savings[1]. That is a tragic commentary on our society. Most people simply fail to start; the mountain looks so high that they never take the first step. They convince themselves that someday they are going to do it, yet they procrastinate indefinitely. Once they get to retirement age, they seek an advisor who can help them make a 20% annual return on their meager portfolio, hoping to make up for the money they failed to save.

Core Truth #7
Everyone Should Have an Emergency Account

One of the most important things you can do is to have an emergency account. Some may wonder why they might need one; after all, wouldn't it be better to put your savings to work in the markets? Why not throw it all into an investment that can be tapped into in case of an emergency?

One reason is you never want to be in a position where you have to liquidate fund assets in an emergency. If you have to do so in a down market, you could easily lose much or all of the growth it took years to accumulate.

An emergency fund, by definition, is money immediately available for an unexpected event: medical expenses, home or car repairs, etc. And, because funds that took years to accumulate can be depleted with the occurrence of one event, you should contribute to your emergency fund on a continual basis.

Core Truth #8
Protect the "Save" in Your Savings Account

This core truth is closely aligned with the need to create an emergency fund. In order to save, you need two separate accounts: one for emergencies, another for saving. The savings account has a one-way door: money goes in but should not come out – it is sacrosanct. It is essential to create a true savings account where the money is saved, not held aside temporarily until a special need arises. If it is raided every time there is an emergency or desire to

1 Employee Benefit Research Institute (EBRI)

buy something, significant savings will never accumulate.

The hardest $10,000 to put into your savings account is often the first $10,000. After that, additional amounts become incrementally easier to put aside and, by the time a person saves $100,000, it snowballs and often starts to grow faster than can be saved. But the first $10,000 is the bogey.

Some people tell me they save regularly. When I ask them how much they put aside each month, a typical response is "We've been saving $350 a month for several years." However, when I ask how much they have in their account, they say something like, "Around $750 dollars." Apparently it is not a savings account. Instead, they have been using it for a spending account to cover the cost of any whim they may have. Make sure you know the difference between your saving and spending accounts, and treat them accordingly.

Core Truth #9
Insure What You Can't Afford to Lose

When purchasing insurance, it's important to differentiate what you can afford to lose and what you can't. Often, people deceive themselves when it comes to illness, misfortune and death. No one gets up thinking, "I might die today," or "I might have an accident and be disabled on the job today," or even, "I could cause a crash and be sued for everything I have today." But not planning for the possibility of those things happening makes us vulnerable to being sucked into a financial black hole from which there is no escape. It is important to insure the things we cannot afford to lose.

Some people abhor the fact that insurance companies make a profit; however, this is not necessarily an evil thing. Our economy needs profitable companies of all kinds so we can grow our wealth as individuals and a society, and insurance companies provide an important product. If you don't believe me, ask the young mother of three children whose husband recently died in a car accident. Without the proceeds from his life insurance policy, she would have been forced to join the ranks of low-income single mothers.

Not being adequately insured is akin to having a retirement plan contingent upon winning a lottery. Conversely, the reason for not insuring something is, quite simply, because you can afford to replace it.

Core Truth #10
Children Need to Know What "Money" Means

Parents must accept responsibility for helping their children understand the role money plays in their lives. If children are not taught some financial basics at an early age, it encourages a lifetime of frustration for them, and has ominous implications for the parents as well.

In addition, many parents spoil their children. They never let them experience failure or pain and, consequently, the children never learn how to deal with the issues they are certain to face as adults. Just as bad, the parents cheat themselves because their children end up living at home far too long, and are a financial drain on their parents. Their kids have no concept of what it means to save to buy something, to be debt free or why it makes a difference. Most lack the financial basics they should have been taught in their teens.

On the other hand, there are children whose parents use an allowance to teach them fundamental lessons about money that they will never forget. If they receive an allowance, it isn't enough to satisfy their every whim. And, once the allowance is spent, they either go without or wait for their next allowance. Throughout their childhood, they are encouraged to work to earn extra money. Their parents have the courage to say "no" when necessary. This changes children for the better.

Living within or beneath one's means may sound like an elementary lesson, but it is one that many Americans, including the leaders of our city, state and federal governments, have not absorbed.

Core Truth #11
Your Choices Affect Multiple Generations

When people hire me as their financial advisor, I believe I have a responsibility to help effect change that will benefit three generations: my clients, the generation below them and the generation above them. Given the small percentage of seniors who retire with sufficient income, many of today's 30- and 40-year-olds will have to help support their parents. In addition, most retirees lack long-term care insurance to help cover the expense of an assisted living facility. Unfortunately, the surging cost of these facilities can destroy the financial stability of several generations.

These financial nightmares, lying dormant in the lives of retirees, can extract a financial and emotional drain that their children may find to be an unbearable burden as well. Early decisions can have a dramatic financial and emotional effect on the lives of both the children and their parents.

Ironically, when I discuss my clients' financial status with them, they invariably want to talk about investment returns. Few have even considered the much larger and potentially more destructive issue of how it will affect them if their parents are unable to be self-sufficient in retirement.

Core Truth #12
An Accurate, Up-to-Date Will or
Trust is Required

Most people understand the importance of having a will. Yet, when I speak to groups of people nearing retirement, more than likely one-third of them have no written financial documents, another third have documents that name the wrong beneficiary – often someone they no longer love, and the rest have ownership designations and other instructions not aligned with their final wishes.

I have reviewed more than 600 financial and estate plans in my career and have yet to see a set of documents where the ownership of assets, beneficiary designations, and other provisions correctly reflect the owner's wishes and true intentions. That is why, prior to creating a will, it is extremely important to conduct a discovery process. A will is not just about the documents, laws and taxes; it's about the people – the ones you love. What can you do to support them? What will make them stronger? How can you ease their burdens during difficult times? Your will is the final statement you will make to the people you care most about. It deserves some serious thoughts about how, why and for whom you are doing it.

Core Truth #13
Find an Advisor Who Will Tell You the Truth

Select a financial advisor who is honest, and willing to tell you things you may not want to hear. For example, "You need to save more or you are not going to be able to retire at 65," or "There is no magic investment that guarantees a 20% return annually."

You may be tempted to choose an advisor who only tells you what you want to hear but you are better off working with an advisor who tells you the truth. What is the truth? Well, if you are basing your retirement projections on earning 20% a year on your investment portfolio and your advisor agrees, you are not being told the truth.

You may have to interview five or ten advisors before you find one who is willing to tell you what you need to hear versus what you would like to hear. And, while many advisors would like you to think they are smarter than the market, know things that haven't yet been priced into the market and, hence, can forecast what is going to happen and advise you accordingly, none of them can.

The most common method for selecting a financial advisor is to ask a friend for a recommendation. However, in all probability the friend hasn't a clue as to whether his or her advisor is competent. More than likely this friend met the advisor through another friend, or because the advisor belonged to the same club or attended the same church. While shared interests or religious beliefs may engender comfort, it is no barometer of professional skill.

The financial advisory business is often more about creating a positive aura than it is about capability. Advisors know that most people want to hear promises of financial results that are all but impossible to attain. They want to avoid the difficult conversations such as saving instead of spending. And, if the advisor gets lucky and is right about the markets, clients think they hired a genius; if wrong, they search for an advisor with a different story.

Core Truth #14
Past Performance is Not an Indicator of Future Potential

Numerous statistical studies have concluded that buying the top-performing investments results in poor returns, principally because today's best performing investments are already over-priced as a result of investors pumping money into them. However, despite a mountain of evidence against it, investors continue to buy the investment products marketers and the media say are doing the best.

Open a magazine and try to find an advertisement for a below-average investment. There are none, of course. Every financial services company has a product that is beating its benchmarks, or so the Wall Street advertisers would have you believe. Often, companies have ads touting one of their products as the best in its class. What they don't mention is that 290 of their 300 products may not be doing so hot.

Shut out the financial pornography (Chart 3.1). It doesn't matter what the advertisements hype or what your friends are doing, all you should be concerned with is what is best for your circumstances, and what you want to do with the rest of your life. Whatever your investment strategy, there will be days, months, even years when your portfolio will be down, and it seems as though everyone else is doing better than you. But it's times like these when it's more important for your investment strategy to be systematic, unemotional and diversified.

Chart 3.1 INVESTMENT PORNOGRAPHY

DEFINITION

Investment Pornography: Investment information designed to appeal to investors' obsessive speculation tendencies.

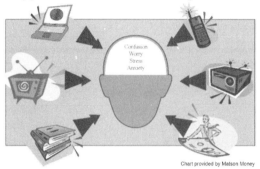

Chart provided by Matson Money

Ignore the financial noise and be confident you have a long-term plan best suited for you.

Core Truth #15
Four Necessities of a Successful Retirement

You should have a strategic focus when working toward your projected retirement that involves four critical elements:

- An emergency fund equal to six months of lifestyle cash flow

- The ability to live on 3% of financial assets

- Five years worth of income in conservative assets

- No debt

These requirements should be built into your plan during the accumulation period, that is, your working years. Whatever level of investment risk tolerance you are comfortable with during your accumulation period, you must eventually carve out five years of conservative assets that you can live on in case the markets spiral downward.

We will discuss these at length later.

Core Truth #16
You Can Be Happy With What You Have

Like most of my clients, I have been blessed to exceed every financial goal I imagined. Had someone told me 30 years ago what my income and net worth would be today, I would have laughed.

No matter how much financial success people achieve, they are always willing to accept more. The question is, "Do you need more to be happy?" If you have not learned to be happy with what you already have, when will you be happy? One of the more difficult challenges for people of means is to be content with their success. Learning to be content will enable you to a live a less stressful life, and do truly memorable things for your family, friends and community.

Core Truth #17
You Don't Know What You Don't Know

You cannot do everything yourself. Overconfidence causes people to do foolish things, and everyone is guilty of faulty thinking in some aspect of their life. Needing professional assistance is not a sign of weakness

People often think they can do a good job investing their own money because they care more about it than anyone else. However, every day they are fed information that reinforces the belief that they can beat the market. They want to believe this and so, not fully understanding the risk they are taking, unwittingly commit financial suicide. After they've lost the bulk of their money, they ask an advisor, "What should I do?" Too late, they are prepared to admit they *don't know what they don't know.*

Core Truth #18
Buy Out Of, Not Into, Bubbles

Investing properly means you will be investing differently than most other people. You will have the most diversified, best-allocated, lowest correlated portfolio of anyone you know. And, at least one-third of the time, your portfolio performance will be worse than those of others.

Unfortunately, most people will buy whatever is hot, even though buying what everyone else is buying has been statistically proven wrong. The majority of investors buy into bubbles when they should be buying into dips. The question is, "Can you handle being different? Can you shut off your emotions and not try to get the best possible return all the time?" If you constantly seek high returns, you are like a dog chasing its own tail around in circles. And, you won't like what you find when you catch it.

You've seen the ubiquitous disclaimer that "past performance is not indicative of future results. The following chart (3.2) is a prime example, depicting how quickly and dramatically top-performing investments can collapse. Calamos Growth A Fund led the pack for a decade, then plummeted to number 595 over the following 24 months.

Chart 3.2 INVESTMENT COMPARISON

INVESTMENT	RANKING	RANKING
	1/1994 - 12/2003	1/2004 - 12/2006
Calamos Growth A	1	595
Vanguard Health Care	2	346
Fidelity Select Electronics	3	974
Fidelity New Millenium	4	606
Alger MidCap Growth Insti 1	5	449
FPA Capital	6	380
Legg Mason Value Prim	7	756
Eaton Vance Worldwide Health Sci A	8	933
Wasatch Core Growth	9	496
Janus Small Cap Val Insti	10	352
Mairs & Power Growth	11	439
Fidelity Select Insurance	12	279
Fidelity Select Home Finance	13	903
Waddell & Reed Adv Science & Tech A	14	207
Royce Low-Priced Stock Service	15	179
PIMCO PEA (aka Allianz OCC)	16	822
Renaissance C	17	913
Thompson Plumb Growth	18	963
Wasatch Ultra WM (aka Principal Inv)	19	96
West Coast Equite A	20	414

Chart provided by Matson Money

Core Truth #19
Current Events Don't Matter

The price of any stock, bond or other investment includes everything the Street already knows about it. Letting current events drive how you invest will throw you into a dark, emotionally charged state where you try to outsmart the people who make their living setting prices.

I'm sure you have heard TV commentators ask a financial analyst what investors should do in light of what happened in the markets that day? As if the analyst knows what is going to happen in the markets tomorrow; as if what they say matters. The only thing that matters is investing prudently for the long-term. You need to be well diversified, have appropriate asset allocation, low market correlation and an academic approach that embraces a long-term strategy.

Core Truth #20
Always Take Advantage of Matching Dollars

I guess there is no polite way to say this. It is just plain stupid not to take matching employer dollars. I have talked to people whose employers match their 401(k) savings dollar for dollar on the first three percent they contribute, yet they still are not saving any money!

Consider this: every $100 a person earns represents $65 or $70 after withholding deductions. Hypothetically, if he or she put that $100 into a 401(k) and if the employer matches it with another $100, he or she would now have $200 invested, versus $65 in take-home pay. That's an immediate return of more than 200%! Where else can they get that kind of return on their money? And, because the money is in an account that grows tax-deferred, it accumulates at an accelerated rate. This means that even in the unlikely event the market tanks and half the savings are lost, our savers will still be okay.

Core Truth #21
Spending Can Become an Addiction

Moneyholism is always nearby. If you doubt it, hop over to Las Vegas and watch the parade of human carnage. To some extent, we are all sinners when it comes to money. We all tend to be guilty of spending money on things we shouldn't. Those who don't have money typically wish they did so they could spend it on something insignificant and likely to depreciate in value. Others start charging unnecessary purchases to their credit cards.

To reach our goals and achieve peace, we have to control the emotions that tempt us to buy things we don't need, things that do little more than cause stress and create emotional damage in our lives. No matter where you are in terms of age, education or wealth, you need to exercise control over spending temptations.

Core Truth #22
Debt is Not Your Friend

Debt may help you to become wealthy, but it also can lead to financial disaster. Some people will use debt to invest in real estate, build a factory or start a business. But debt causes more people to go broke than to get rich. Debt is a tool to be used with great caution. It is not your friend. At best, it is a necessary evil. In addition, the risk of being in debt is that, when things go wrong, you can lose everything.

If you have no debt, you will still be financially secure when bad things happen. Being debt-free is a vital part of attaining financial success.

Core Truth #23
A Good Life is a Simple Life

You can be healthier and happier if you remove the things in your life that create stress. Have you ever noticed that, in general, people in poorer nations tend to smile more than Americans? Could it be because they lead simpler lives?

Often, people have visions of building a perfect life around the acquisition of properties, airplanes, wardrobes or vintage automobiles. However, possessions can create needless complications and stress. Life is best lived when it is based on simplicity and finding contentment in what we have. While highly successful people can afford to purchase whatever they want; they can only be truly happy if they don't *need* anything.

A simple life does not mean you have to deny yourself everything you need and enjoy; however, it does consist of not buying something just to maintain an image or to keep up with someone else. Simplifying your life not only helps reduce stress, it frees up more time for you to spend with family and friends, enjoy nature, and to pursue worthwhile, fulfilling experiences.

Core Truth #24
Now is the Time to Develop a Financial Plan

If you have not already done so, find the time and motivation to develop a financial plan and, then, commit to implementing it. For some people, creating a financial plan is like asking them to eat an elephant. It looks so big they don't know where to start. However, by taking one bite at a time, eventually they will have eaten the elephant. Similarly, creating a long-term saving goal often appears so overwhelming that many people never take the first step. As a result, when the day comes that they need money, there is none … they didn't even take the first step.

The elephant is always in the room during the time you should be accumulating money. For example, if your goal is to accumulate $100,000 in 10 years for your child's college tuition, you may never get started because the amount seems unattainable. Rather than anguishing about something 10 years in the future, simply take the first bite of the elephant, trusting that your financial plan will get you where you need to be when that day arrives.

Make sure you are saving in the savings bucket, not the spending bucket. You can't save for long-term goals in a checking account or Christmas Fund. Instead, your savings needs to be put in an account you don't touch until you need it for the events or items you are saving for.

Core Truth #25
Investment Products Aren't Good or Bad

There are no inherently good or bad investment products. There are appropriate and inappropriate applications for every legitimate investment product.

Some people condemn annuities as a terrible investment, primarily because of the sales commissions and annual expenses associated with the products. Those who support annuities point to their value in helping protect against outliving one's assets. As an advisor, I can make a compelling case for either side of the argument, depending on the individual's circumstances. And that's exactly the point, whether annuities, equities, ETFs or any other financial product. They must be used in the proper application.

Core Truth #26
Financial Storms Will Come ... Again

We will always have financial storms of one kind or another. The only defense is a plan and process that is systematic, unemotional and diversified. Remember, the plan is the critical element, not the investment returns. The process, not the investment choices, dictates the results. No one knows when the next storm will arrive, only that it will come. The one thing we can control is the process.

The late comedian Sam Kinnison told a story about volcanic eruptions that destroyed a nearby village every few years. A survivor standing on a pile of ashes proclaimed, "We will rebuild!" Kinnison asked, "Don't they get it?"

The financial markets are similarly volatile and unpredictable. No one can tell you whether tomorrow's market will soar or collapse because no one knows what will happen tomorrow. No one has that information. Yet, despite the fact that most rational people recognize this, they still ignore common sense as they continue chasing investment returns. They are oblivious to the perils posed by the next financial storm. Lacking a solid plan exposes you to the vagaries of the markets and the economy. Not surprisingly, when the volcano erupts yet again, if you don't have a plan and a process you will be helpless to defend yourself.

In the following chapters, I will discuss the powerful influence these myths and core truths have on the way people make decisions about saving, spending and managing their finances.

♦♦♦

4

The Accumulation Phase

"We need to plan for success, and we need to help our children understand the need to start accumulating money, creating good habits and having a plan or purpose for their money as soon as possible."

– Wayne von Borstel

The accumulation period is the most critical phase of our financial lives. The attitudes, habits and discipline developed during the 40 years that the average American spends working for a living will determine whether the rest of one's life will be fulfilling or unsatisfactory. Sadly, the vast majority of people living in the richest nation in the history of mankind will experience the latter.

Just as most people fail to plan for the day they will die, despite knowing it will inevitably arrive, most Americans reach retirement age in a sorry financial state because they failed to take the time to develop a reliable financial plan. Knowing that the actions they take during the accumulation period of their lives will determine whether they can retain their human dignity during the final 20 or 30 years of their lives, it is inconceivable anyone would postpone creating a viable retirement plan for even a day.

But postpone and procrastinate they do. There is always time, but there is never time. Days turn into weeks, and weeks into years. One day they wake up and are no longer 25 years old and carefree. Instead, they are 55 or 65, ready to stop working and enjoy life, but they can't because they don't have enough money. They did not listen to the right messages, and instead they tried to find happiness by buying automobiles, timeshares, jewelry, furniture and boats. Even when they made a half-hearted attempt to invest for retirement, they bought into the Wall Street marketing mantra. They were convinced they would not have to give up their spending addiction if they bought this or that investment product that would generate large investment returns and allow them to sail off into the retirement sunset on their new yacht.

What is going on in our society when families can't save $300 a month to assure their financial future, but they can spend $500 a month leasing a new SUV every three years?

Most people I talk to have such a distorted perception of how much money they will need to live comfortably after they retire; it truly frightens me. No one has told them the truth nor forced them to confront reality. While the truth is sometimes unpleasant or inconvenient, it is essential to help change attitudes and spending habits that are deeply ingrained.

When conversing with other advisors, I rarely hear any of them say they have candid conversations with their clients regarding these issues. Advisors or brokers working for an employer, regardless of how they are compensated, often find it is difficult to be completely frank with their clients. Instead, they are more inclined to tell them what they want to hear. It is easier to reassure clients that they do not have to make any substantial attitude or spending changes to reach their financial goals. They are told they can still achieve financial success if they allow the advisor to utilize stock-picking skills to beat the market averages, and this will make additional saving unnecessary. Easy.

For advisors, that's the way to keep clients from having to make hard choices and to keep them in the fold. Let them think everything will be all right. No sweat. Tell them what they want to hear so they can go home and continue their moneyholic behavior. Unfortunately, advisors who risk telling clients the truth — they need a solid plan that includes saving more and spending less — may lose clients to other advisors who will tell them there is no need to sacrifice, no need to change and no need to worry. Sound familiar?

In the real world it doesn't work this way and, usually, it doesn't matter whether the client earns $50,000 or $500,000 a year. Without a reliable plan, the amount of money someone earns during a lifetime is irrelevant in terms of having a rewarding retirement. The wealthy make more money, but spend more because they have more expensive homes and hobbies. Most wealthy people lack the ability to live cheaply because they have never had to. They are ill-prepared for a lifestyle downgrade in retirement, yet many find themselves forced to do just that. It is not a pleasant task having to tell an elderly couple who thought themselves immune to financial sacrifice that they cannot afford to spend the way they have for the past 40 years. It's heartbreaking, and I don't want that to happen to my clients.

Getting Started

During the accumulation phase of your life, almost anything you do to save money will work out provided you have a plan, make disciplined save/spend decisions and, most important, do not delay getting started.

Too many people get caught up in planning analysis paralysis. They overthink the investment side of the equation and forget to get started with systematic saving. Debating which investments to choose is almost irrelevant for someone just beginning to save. There are literally thousands to choose from. Instead, they just need to get into the habit of saving until they have accumulated a sufficient enough amount that the choice of which fund or other investment to buy becomes meaningful.

Chart 4.1 TYPES OF INVESTMENTS

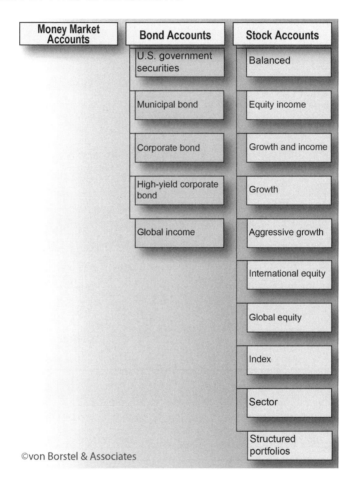

©von Borstel & Associates

Six Excuses to Postpone Saving

Financial success has zero percent correlation to how much a person earns; it has one hundred percent correlation to how much a person saves. Following are six excuses I often hear from people for not saving.

1.

I don't make enough money.

People say they would save more if they earned more. While they may actually believe that, in my experience big earners tend to reach their goals less often than those who make less because they do not take saving as seriously. Those who make a lot of money must save a lot in order to preserve their lifestyle in later years. It is easy for them to make money, so they believe they can always make more. Often they have less discipline when it comes to spending and less urgency when it comes to saving.

2.

I have enough for retirement.

Many people don't have any idea how much they will need in retirement to maintain their current lifestyles. Some may say they already have enough for retirement. Enough what? If they don't even know what they will need, and have not measured the statistical probability of accumulating sufficient money for retirement, how do they know they have enough? Often they don't knoRew how hard their money is working for them, or how much they need to be putting away for retirement. So what is the likelihood they will have enough? They may fool themselves by saying, "I'm okay," but they are whistling in the dark. Even if someone has created a financial plan for them, chances are no one has helped them accurately measure their chances of failure, and most of them haven't even considered the possibility of failure.

There are three things that are certain to happen during retirement and some perhaps several times:

- Inflation will exceed 10%
- Markets will drop 20% or more
- Personal health will go sideways

These are all random but statistically inevitable occurrences. They may strike the year after you retire, five or ten years later, or a month before you die. Your age when they strike, and how well you have planned and invested your money, will determine if you have a satisfying retirement and if you die with at least a dollar in your pocket.

As a financial coach and advisor, I find it frustrating that our industry, as a whole, does such a poor job educating people about what they need to know. Financial firms design impressive brochures that talk about the retirement "Red Zone," the need for life insurance, college savings plans and other topics designed to sell their products, but they fail to provide financial education during the accumulation period when it is possible for people to actually do something to prepare for retirement.

3. *I will start saving when I'm older.*

The way financial marketers try to generate excitement about investing during the critical years just before retirement, or during what is known as the retirement red zone, is both laughable and disingenuous. While it is never too late to save for retirement, waiting until five years before retirement to start planning with the hope that you can accumulate enough money to last the rest of your life is a terribly misleading strategy.

One might argue that red zone marketing will motivate someone who has not saved anything for retirement to get started. However, wouldn't it be better if marketers encouraged people to start saving in their 20s instead of waiting five years before they expect to retire? This would be a win-win situation for everyone concerned. Product providers, investment brokers and financial advisors would get more money to invest and to help people reach a successful retirement. Investors would pay fewer taxes, have fewer social problems and experience less stress in their lives. And, most importantly, they would be better prepared for retirement, live happier, more fulfilling lives and, overall, become more generous contributors to society.

Instead, many firms promote the red zone message: "Let's get serious now that retirement is fast approaching." It's a sales gimmick that offers false hope and unrealistic expectations and is fashioned to sell product, pure and simple. It doesn't convey what is best for you or for society; it's a losing strategy. But, by pretending they have a strategy to salvage retirement for people who have spent the past 35 years spending every dollar they made, Wall Street peddlers sell more products. Unfortunately, at age 60 it's too late for any practical investment strategy to make a significant difference during retirement, although some firms spend millions to convince people otherwise.

Unfortunately, Wall Street is also sending a subliminally deceptive message to younger people that there is no need to start saving today. After all, why bother making financial sacrifices early in life if the great Wall Street money machine can bail you out when you're 60?

You might compare saving early to someone rolling a snowball down a steep hill. The first 20 feet or so there is not much change or speed. But by the time it nears the bottom of the hill, the snowball is so big and moving so fast it will flatten you if you get in its way. For people starting out, saving $100 or $200 a month can be boring and appear to accomplish next to nothing. But 20 or 30 years later, those small monthly contributions made in the first few years are probably worth more than all the additional money saved since.

Below, Chart 4.2 shows the drastic effect delaying saving for retirement for only one year can have on your retirement income – $34,357. That's $3,084 less income annually or $257 less monthly.

Chart 4.2 PROCRASTINATION: THE GREATEST RETIREMENT RISK

Monthly investment	$500
Starting age	45
Ending age	65
Ending value	$333,943

Monthly investment	$500
Starting age	46
Ending age	65
Ending value	$299,586

Cost of delay	$34,357
Reduction in monthly retirement income	$257

Return based on the assumption that $500 is invested at the first of each month and earns a 9% return annually. This chart is not based on any particular investment. ©von Borstel & Associates

People need to start saving as early as possible, and Wall Street firms need to help young adults measure and cultivate what they will need for retirement. Money in retirement means choices. And, while money cannot make you happy, lack of money *will* make you unhappy. Money gives you the freedom to make palatable choices during retirement.

I need to pay off my debt first.

When I entered the financial services industry three decades ago, I was instructed to help people pay off their debt and build an emergency fund so they could begin to invest. However, for most people, if they waited until they were debt-free to start investing they never started. Once they paid off their debt, the first thing most of them did was to create more debt. Unfortunately, the average person feels comfortable living with debt. Even when they eliminate their debt and save $10,000-$15,000 they start thinking about buying things they really don't need ... again! They are addicted to debt.

Surprisingly, the issue of debt affects people at all levels of income. Most people haven't learned to be happy with what they have. They are constantly creating more debt because they believe the things they purchase will bring them happiness, whether a bigger or better home, car, furniture, jewelry, vacations or gifts.

A few years ago, a married couple I know sold their business at an enormous profit and immediately bought a huge home, complete with swimming pool, on a lake with a private dock. Of course, having a dock meant they needed a boat. They couldn't decide between a speedboat and a luxury cruiser so they bought both, which meant they had to expand the dock. The house was more than 6,000 square feet and none of their old furniture looked quite right in the new place, so they went shopping again. They financed everything with minimum down payments so they could hang onto most of their cash. However, vacations, a new wine cellar and extravagant gifts to their children eroded their savings. In less than two years they found they needed more than $20,000 each month to meet their living costs and debt. They were living on the edge. Their lives were full of stress and their marriage was in trouble as they constantly argued about money. Both of them had to go back to work at a time when they should have been worry free. Instead, their lives were caving in on them. None of the things they bought brought them happiness or contentment. They were actually happier when they were struggling to build the business together and living in a pleasant little bungalow – boatless and dockless.

Like drug addicts, every time moneyholics buy something, the next time they must buy something bigger and more costly to get the same fix. The deceptively simple solution to this money merry-go-round is to learn to be happy with what you have and who you are. Once you can do this, you have the potential to build tremendous real wealth.

5.

I can earn more by investing my money than by saving it.

For many investors, the concept of putting money into an emergency fund or savings account that earns little or no interest makes no sense. Young people are particularly impatient when it comes to lazy dollars. If money they set aside doesn't grow quickly, they often lose interest, ignoring the long-term benefits of saving.

However, an emergency fund and savings account allow you to invest the rest of your money without concerns about restrictions or penalties. You may never need to access your emergency fund, and in today's environment you probably won't earn much, if any, interest on it. However, because you have it, your other money can be invested more aggressively, be more tax advantaged, and can lock in at a higher long-term rate of return. The most important thing to remember is the total portfolio will earn more and, when things go wrong, there is no need to liquidate portfolio holdings at a disadvantageous time, pay withdrawal penalties or dismantle the long-term portfolio strategy. While it is often difficult for investors to get their minds around the concept, once they understand how lazy dollars in an emergency fund and a savings account help hold the pieces of their financial plan together, it all makes sense.

6.

I can live on less once I retire, so I really won't need to save much money.

People kid themselves about retirement, about how much they will need to maintain the lifestyle they have grown accustomed to. However, more than likely they can't keep up with their debt right now, much less after they stop working. Perhaps they think something will happen between now and retirement that will take care of their needs, although they have no idea what that something will be. They believe it will all work out ... somehow. And if it doesn't, well, they can live on half of what they spend now. Or, at least, that's what they tell themselves.

Unfortunately, it just doesn't work that way. Those who are moneyholics during their working years will still be moneyholics after they retire. They need to cure their spending addictions now. They need to plan and to save.

Many people look for reasons not to do these things. They don't want to put money into an emergency fund, and they sure as heck don't want to give up their spending habits because they are having so much fun spending everything they earn. However, their chances of having enough money for a comfortable retirement are about the same as those of winning a lottery. Perhaps a lottery win is what they are counting on to fund their retirement.

Speaking the Same Language

Financial success is the result of starting with a solid plan. This is repetitious, but I repeat it for a reason: it is vital. Expecting to reach your financial goals without a plan is akin to building a house without a blueprint. Lacking specific and accurate measurements, you will never get your financial house constructed properly. An important step in that construction is making certain you and your advisor, your financial contractor if you will, speak the same language and interpret the details of your blueprint in precisely the same way.

Both of you must clearly understand what the other one means and what you are agreeing to when it comes to critical considerations, such as your investment strategy and risk tolerance. While this may not sound difficult to do, during the many years I have spoken at conferences and adult financial education classes, rarely have I found anyone who can accurately describe their investment strategy. They might say they are conservative, moderately aggressive or opportunistic investors. However, their description typically mimics the terminology used by whoever created their portfolio. Most people really don't know what it means, yet they think they do. Rarely does their portfolio composition reflect their description. Alarmingly, the two are often dissimilar.

As an investor responsible for your own financial future, you need to be sure you and your advisor are using the same financial vocabulary and that you both mean the same thing. For example, you must have a clear understanding of the risk level in your portfolio, not merely some vague term that sounds like it reflects your concept of risk.

Understanding Risk

However you describe it, your designated level of risk involves a specific standard deviation. You can expect your portfolio returns to fluctuate roughly double whatever that number is the majority of the time, and sometimes even more. You must be prepared for this level of ebb and flow or you will short circuit when it happens. If you know in advance what to expect and understand that the variance is normal market activity, you can deal with it. It's the unknown that can traumatize you. As an industry, financial advisors avoid talking about this because they are afraid people won't invest if they do.

There will be years you think your strategy is brilliant, and other years you may want to jump out the window. It is important to understand that there is a vortex of returns and that it is possible to either lose 30% or gain 30% in any given year. Knowing and accepting this will allow you to remain confident because you know in advance what can happen, you just do not know when.

The longer your time frame, the longer that vortex of unpredictable returns continues, getting you that much closer to average and predictable returns. Just be aware that in any given year, or any given three- to five-year period, returns will not be at all "normal" or predictable. However, I believe if you have a sound strategy that accurately reflects your risk tolerance, you will know that, over the long term, all those seemingly erratic returns will average out. By understanding the risk and having patience, you can endure the waves thrown up against your retirement boat and sail past them to the horizon without getting seasick, losing your head and jumping overboard. See Chart 2.4 on page 18 for an example.

The chart below (4.3) is a framework for the decision process of choosing an investment.

Chart 4.3 INVESTMENT VS. RISK DECISION TREE

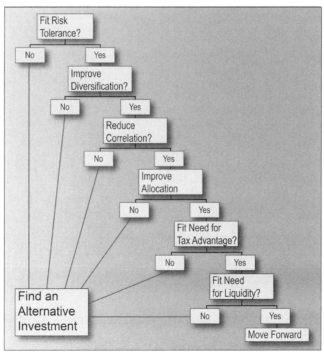

© von Borstel & Associates

Higher Risk Equals Higher Risk

Many investors buy into the myth that taking additional risk will yield higher returns. But there is a point when the level of risk becomes bungee jumping. It can be exciting, but bad things can happen. Taking imprudent risk in the pursuit of investment returns, more often than not, has just the opposite effect. It diminishes potential returns. There are certain immutable laws of investing based on fundamental academics. Ignoring those laws and taking unnecessary risk is usually the result of someone waiting too long to start saving and then thinking they can make up for lost time by rolling the dice. Maybe they will get lucky and hit the jackpot, but chances of that happening are slim.

Often, when someone does get lucky, they tell everyone they know, and so does the broker who put them into the investment. Others hear about it and think the same will happen for them. However, for most the result is merely more losses that put them even further away from reaching their retirement goals. No matter when you start to accumulate money for retirement, you must understand and mitigate risk.

Being aggressive does not mean being stupid, or following the lemmings because everyone else seems to be doing it. I don't know where the lemmings will land, but it isn't worth the risk to find out. That is why you must distill the academic measurement of a portfolio, understand what it means and determine what is normal for that level of risk.

Individual Stocks are Best

Often, investors get hooked on buying stocks. They hear a good story from someone "in the know" and they just cannot resist. They are convinced someone out there must have the inside track and knows what stocks will go up and when. People love the idea of beating Wall Street at its own game. They want to "beat the big boys" so badly, they will take risks far in excess of what is sensible. They love the excitement, the gamble, and the thought of a potential windfall.

However, when taking these risks they often fail to adequately diversify. They have little or no idea what is going on inside the companies whose stocks they buy. They don't know if the CEO is sick, a thief or will die in a plane crash next week. They don't know what the competitors of these companies are planning, whether Congress is about to pass a bill that will gut their market share, or if the company will become politically incorrect and get taxed out of existence. They don't have a clue as to what economic event, political preference, inappropriate behavior or chance occurrence will decimate these companies. Instead, they buy the stocks because they like the story they hear. It's like looking at a hot new exotic car: it's just so sexy and exciting, they have to have one.

Excitement is not a good reason to invest, nor is the satisfaction of trying to beat the people on Wall Street. The only sound reason to invest is because you are trying to build wealth and attain your dream. If you find you can't resist the excitement, take some mad money you won't miss if it is lost, and invest it in some stocks you like. If you lose it, you haven't decapitated your finances. Just remember, you must build your future based on a prudent plan, not chasing the next hot stock.

The Value of Long-Term Investing

Financial professionals often talk about the importance of "long-term return on investment." That's fine, except that the holding period for the average mutual fund investor is 3.5 years or less. When people take their money out of an investment, it's usually because they are dissatisfied with the returns, so they invest it somewhere else. Continuous investment "hopscotching" is why many people never reach their goals.

Everyone talks about long-term investing, but most people lack the patience for it. They think whatever they have may not be as good as what they just heard about on CNN or from their broker. Jumping from one investment strategy to another every few years is a sure recipe for failure. Each time it's like starting over again. The only way the long-term averages can work for you is to choose an investment style that is prudent and academically predictable, and leave it alone! Yes, the first year or any other year may be a down market; but over the long haul, the averages will prevail. They always have. Shifting your strategy every time there is a down year

65

will only lead to higher risk with less chance of financial success. Create a prudent plan, stay with it, ignore the financial porn, and you have the best chance of getting where you want to go.

Here's an example of financial porn:

> *Today, the chief strategist for a major Wall Street firm explained in an interview that he's worried investors now view the stock market as a casino and that "We have to do something to change that perception." The reporter's very next question is, "What stocks can you recommend to our viewers right now?" The strategist responds, "One stock I can confidently recommend today is eBay ..."*

Well, thanks for the hot stock tip. That should certainly help change people's perception of the market as a casino. How nice that the folks on Wall Street are so committed to mending their ways.

The Best Accumulation Investment

There is no product that is the "best" for everyone. Companies touting their product as the best have no idea whether their mass marketing appeal is being heard by someone who is 30 or 60 years of age. Nor do they know the specific needs or goals of anyone upon whose eyes or ears their messages fall. They don't know if the person they are pitching has a solid financial plan or is winging it. In short, they don't know anything about the people to whom they are promoting their products. The only thing they do know is that they have product to sell and the best way to do it is to make it sound exciting and sexy, and to convince people it is the best investment for everyone.

Instead of listening to the hype and hoping to find a magic formula, investors should be setting priorities. What is the best use of their money that will allow them to reach their goals? Instead of chasing performance, they should be asking, "What might happen that could prevent me from reaching my goals? What could happen that would hurt me the most?"

For example, people who save their money and plan well but fail to buy health insurance can lose everything in a moment due to illness or an accident. I had a son who lived less than 30 days. The medical expenses far exceeded what I would have paid for a lifetime of health premiums. If I had not had health insurance when Nicholas was born, my wife and I would have lost everything.

When people are young, healthy, in love and feeling invincible, they often question the need for seemingly unnecessary things like health insurance. Needless to say, you cannot afford to take the risk.

It is never a question of what is the best investment; it is always a question of what investments best fit your individual needs, choices and priorities. Rarely is it a single investment, but rather a combination of investments, insurance, saving and documents that provide the glue for your financial puzzle. Your approach should be to find the proper combination of financial products and wrap it around your individual needs.

Every time you make a financial decision there are side affects to be considered, such as liquidity, tax consequences, diversification, excessive risk, or inflation. It is almost like taking medications without considering the impact one prescription can have on another. Your financial advisor needs to help you create a balanced portfolio, taking into consideration how each element will affect your long-term financial prognosis.

I don't have any two clients with the same financial plan or portfolio because no two people have identical needs, goals or financial DNA. Each is different, so my goal is to find the pieces that make up their individual financial puzzles, the combination of financial products that best meet the needs of their financial DNA.

Teaching Children About Money

Children tend to emulate the spending habits of their parents. If you are a moneyholic, chances are your children will be afflicted with the same addiction. Children who are taught the value of money at an early age have a better chance of becoming self-sufficient, responsible adults. They are also far less likely to take up residence on their retired parent's couch as middle-aged laggards.

Too many young people are not given the opportunity by their parents to suffer financially. They grow up thinking money is for spending, and that's what they do. What happens when someone in our country pays off an automobile loan? Typically, they immediately go out and buy a new one and go right back into debt. To me, a car is four tires and a steering wheel to get me from point A to point B; the rest is just emotion. If I could convince young people to forego just one car purchase in their 20s, it would completely change their life.

If, as your advisor, I asked you to convince your 25-year-old son or daughter to borrow $30,000 and put the entire amount into the stock market, you would say I was crazy and probably fire me. Yet the average American thinks it's perfectly fine for their child to borrow $30,000 and buy a depreciating asset that will be worthless in 10 years if it doesn't kill them first. Now consider the Rule of 72: money earning 7% annually doubles every 10 years. Historically, the market returns an average of about 12% annually, which means money doubles every six years. So let's assume you talk your 25-year-old into borrowing $30,000 and investing it in the market. I have no idea what the market will do next year or any other year, but let's assume your offspring resists the urge to take the money out and buy something, and instead leaves it in the market until he or she is ready to retire at age 65, some 40 years from now. Using the long-term market averages, that nest egg will have increased to roughly $4 million by the time your child is ready to retire! At 10% annual return in retirement, that amount will generate roughly $33,000 monthly income for the rest of their life. All for skipping just one new car purchase. And by the way, when your child dies, there will be a substantial amount remaining to pass on to future generations or a worthy charity. Given that 70% of the 25-year-olds in the richest country in world are broke the day they retire, that crazy idea doesn't seem so crazy anymore, does it?[1]

What You Do Today Affects Tomorrow

Despite what you may hear, the last decade has not been the worst in the last century. Take a look at some of the headlines back in the

---

1 Remember, investments in securities may result in loss of principle. Past performance is no assurance of future results.

1930s and 1940s – the Great Depression, the early days of WW II. Those were truly frightening times.

Today, people are often thrown off course by our over-reactive media. They have also been sold a bill of goods by the political establishment. Making excuses for everything that happens, they over-blow the potential consequences, telling everyone that only they, in their wisdom, can save them.

However, no one knows what the future holds, but even if it turns out to be tougher than it was in the past, all it means is that it's even more critical to acquire prudent habits and have a solid plan that will help us be unemotional, systematic and diversified. Without a plan, we are vulnerable to every media pseudo-disaster. Without a plan we lose confidence in our future and revert to being emotional animals making irrational financial decisions. We start to believe the ominous predictions of the news media, people who know nothing more about the future than we do.

Fifty years ago, sound financial planning was the best defense against an uncertain future. Today, sound planning is still the best defense. And I suspect 50 years from now, it still will be. I don't imagine the media will get noisier or offer worse advice; I can't imagine politicians will be more inept or arrogant; but the core truths will still be as beneficial, compelling and applicable as they always have been. It's one thing we can rely on.

Someone has to stand up today and articulate what is right and true, both in the life we are living and the future life we visualize. We need clarity surrounding the reality of where we are now and what we hope and dream about, a realistic linkage between our present and our future. What we do today will affect what happens tomorrow.

Freedom to Pursue Happiness and Success

No one is entitled to anything, except the freedom to do his or her best and to succeed or fail. One of the great things about our country is that people are allowed to fail. It is what makes our system strong. Nobody is entitled to success or happiness. We can plan for it, earn it, and by maintaining a positive attitude, we are bound to achieve better results than if we become negative and quit trying. We may not get everything we want, but that's okay as long as we do our best. If you plan to be mediocre, you will be. If you plan to be great, you may be, or you may only be mediocre. But you can never be happy if you plan to fail, think you are entitled, or expect someone else to take care of you.

We should all plan for success and do our best to make a difference. We live in the greatest country in the world where we are able to seize opportunities, take reasonable risks, work hard, overcome obstacles, suffer the inevitable setbacks, and still grow as individuals.

In today's economic environment, it will probably be harder for our children and grandchildren to accumulate money. Because of this, they need to start sooner. Financial planning will be critical because their generations will likely be taxed more heavily, have fewer employment opportunities available and will face increasingly stronger global competition. It will be harder for them to earn enough to save what they need for retirement.

In addition, in today's politic climate companies are often labeled as evil and there is hostility toward productive people in profitable businesses. Profits are being demonized. However, companies are merely collections of working people and stockholders trying to make money. In our society, companies that make profits and pay taxes provide the money for the things politicians want to spend it on. Unfortunately, they are often vilified for their success.

The game is changing, at least for the time being. However, over the long haul free markets will go where the money is, whether here in the USA or elsewhere. If businesses can't make money here, they will take their wealth somewhere else.

Eventually we will come out of our economic malaise, and the evil stigma currently attached to productivity and profits will dissipate and life will be good. However, whatever happens, we need to plan for success, and we need to help our children understand the need to start accumulating money, creating good habits and having a plan or purpose for their money as soon as possible. It's our responsibility as parents and as a society.

◆◆◆

5

The Transitional Phase

"By having a transition focus, you can reach your true potential. You can have peace of mind and a rewarding and satisfying late life."

– Wayne von Borstel

As we approach retirement, our focus should begin to transition from an emphasis on accumulation to the issues surrounding retirement.

This period has been dubbed by some companies as the *Red Zone*, a metaphor no doubt intended to portray a time of increased emphasis on accumulation. However, the unintended imagery conjures up a battleground's bloody aftermath. And, for the financially unprepared, the battleground is a more accurate description.

An entire book could be written about the reasons financial product firms invented the red zone misnomer, and why they would like us to believe that the final few years before retirement represent a dangerous and potentially critical period that calls for an abrupt change in both planning and investment strategy. However, while there may be some minor tweaking required, the concept that this period calls for a strategic upheaval is little more than marketing hype. It's the last chance for the folks on Wall Street to sell some financial products. But people don't need financial products; they need financial solutions.

As mentioned previously, if you have waited until three- to five-years before you intend to retire to start thinking about what you are doing to prepare, it's probably too late. In the previous chapters we've listed things you need to do in the years leading up to retirement, things that can help ensure you are in a good position the day you retire. These issues need to be actively addressed as early as possible.

The red zone was created as a framework for selling some sexy new products to meet the need of late starters ... the red zone razzle dazzle, if you will. However, these years are better spent refocusing and fine-tuning your financial plan, not chasing returns in an effort to make up for lost time. This is a time for following through on the financial plan and thought process you created the day you started saving for retirement (ideally when you were in your 20s), with a few minor adjustments.

Health First

As you approach retirement, your first concern should be your health. If you intend to retire before age 65, your most pressing need is to secure comprehensive, renewable health insurance. Often, the people I talk to at seminars indicate they intend to retire before they are 65 and when they are eligible for federal health coverage. I try to emphasize that they can't afford to go a single day during that period without health insurance. One bad heart tick and they could lose everything they have saved over their lifetime. That's not an acceptable risk.

Many manage to convince themselves that bad things won't happen to them. Meanwhile, they ignore the statistical probability that one out of three of them will be out of work for at least 90 days at least once in their working years as a result of accident or illness. A 2010 study by the nonprofit LIFE Foundation[1] revealed that 49% of working Americans would have trouble meeting their financial obligations after only 30 days should they be unable to work. And, a startling 74% said they would face financial trouble within six months. (You may recall my previous comments about the necessity of an emergency fund. Here's another example of why it's so important.)

When the economy sinks, disability insurance becomes even more of an afterthought for the majority of Americans. As evidenced by another statistic from the LIFE study, roughly two-thirds of Americans felt less financially secure in 2010 than they did a year earlier, and only 17% worried about the financial threat of becoming disabled and being unable to work. Their greatest concerns were being unable to keep up with bills (55%), losing money in investments and savings (34%), and being laid off (20%).

This pervasive mindset reinforces the rationalization that accidents and illnesses only happen to other people. I often hear, "I eat right, I exercise, and I take a cholesterol drug so I'm fine." Unfortunately, seemingly

Too many people fall prey to relying on COBRA insurance to carry them through until they can secure permanent health insurance. COBRA is a stopgap policy; but often people treat it as an 18-month health security blanket. Failing to promptly acquire sustainable health insurance, they suffer a serious health setback and find themselves unable to qualify for or afford permanent insurance. The older a person is, the more likely they are to be hit with an illness, and the less time they have to try to recoup financially. It's an avoidable disaster yet it happens all the time. Families can be destroyed, both financially and emotionally, as a result.

1 LIFE Survey; Conducted by Kelton Research; April 14-21, 2010; Life and Health Insurance Foundation for Education (LIFE Foundation)

healthy people have had heart attacks and dropped dead while jogging. The chances of that occurring are small, but there's no guarantee it won't happen to you or your spouse.

You cannot afford to let an occurrence such as this devastate your financial plan. A single occurrence can put you so far behind you may never catch up. That's why it is crucial that you have health and disability insurance depending on your goals, resources and plan requirements.

Financial Test Drive

Most people who respond to what is being said in this book are already financially successful to a greater or lesser degree. Most have made good choices, done the right things, saved for retirement and accumulated some wealth. What they may lack is a clear understanding of the income they will need to support the lifestyle they have in mind for their retirement.

People often give me estimates of what they think they can live on in retirement without any real measurement or basis for those numbers. To help them find out if they are being realistic, I suggest they practice living on that amount for a year. Most know they can't do it.

Here's a simple method for estimating your income needs: total your current take-home pay (after deductions) and subtract the amount currently being set aside for other savings plans and disability insurance (you won't be paying these after retirement). Let's say this comes to $7,000 monthly. Now deduct the amounts you will be spending less on during retirement, such as gasoline, commuting expenses, work clothing and the like. Then add in the cost of the things you plan to do when you retire. Many people say they plan to travel. Others plan to join a golf club, or build a dream home. Remember to allow for increased healthcare costs. You can also take into consideration that most people spend significantly less in their 80s than they do in their 60s. As they age, they tend to buy less, eat less, travel less and become less active. While they can still have enjoyable lives, they just don't need to spend as much. So it's probably okay to assume you can live on 20-30% less once you reach your 80s.

This exercise will give you a clearer picture of what you will need during retirement. It will help you determine whether or not you have enough wealth to live as planned and to be able to do the things you want. For most people, it's a genuine wake-up call.

You will recall the four retirement requirements previously discussed:

- An emergency fund equal to six months of lifestyle cash-flow.
- The ability to live on 3% of financial assets
- Five years worth of income in conservative assets
- No debt

Once you have an idea of how much money you will need for retirement, it's important to measure whether you are on target to meet that number. Here are four major factors to consider:

- When do I plan to retire?
- How much income will I need?
- How much wealth do I have now?
- How hard is it working for me?

The intersection of these factors will give you a number that predicts the probability of retirement success based on your existing resources. This measurement shows what the chances are of you running out of money before you die. It's a critical assessment. Few people know their statistical chance of going broke before death. It's like jumping out a plane with no parachute, hoping for something soft to cushion their landing. Most people haven't made allowances for the three variables likely to make the biggest impact on their retirement: inflation going up, the markets going down and their health going sideways.

You must measure the random chance of running out of money

while you are focused on transition, and you need to know what that number is so you can make intellectual versus emotional decisions regarding retirement. A lot of people end up making emotional decisions based on frustration, anger or fatigue. They are tired of the work grind, the commute, office politics or the responsibility of running a business. They hate their boss, being on their feet all day, the travel and abusive customers. Many are physically and psychologically drained and highly motivated to retire. The question then becomes whether or not they are being financially responsible. Chances are that no one has helped them to accurately assess that question, and people in the financial industry are often all too willing to tell them what they want to hear. "Sure you can afford to retire." But if they measure carefully, many will find they have a 40-50% chance of running out of resources. No one wants to hear that. That's why it is vital to create a realistic budget.

Staying the Course

Often, as people approach retirement, they think they have to shift to a more conservative investment strategy. However, a lot of people run out of money before they die by following this advice, because inflation eats away at their purchasing power.

Chart 5.1 THE RISING COST OF AUTOS AND HOMES

	1970	1990	2010	2030
Auto	$3,708	$14,489	$28,415	$78,659
Home	$26,600	$149,800	$272,900	$874,106

Average costs for homes and autos between 1970 and 2010. 2030 costs are projections only.
Sources: www1.eere.energy.gov, & www.census.gov   ©von Borstel & Associates

Let's assume for a moment you bought your first new car in 1975, a time when you could have owned a sporty little Mustang for around $4,000; a flashy Oldsmobile Delta 88 Royale for $5,200; or a Jaguar E Type convertible (with a V-12 engine no less) for about $8,800. Those same cars cost about ten times that amount today, except for the Oldsmobile, which died in 2004. Retirees who don't take into account the enormous impact inflation has on their purchasing power might be surprised to wake up one morning in the future to discover an apple costs $10. When that happens, the fate of the Oldsmobile might be preferable to not being able to write a check for food.

Take a long look at the chart below (5.2). I call it the "Do You Feel Lucky" analysis. It illustrates the critical importance of both the portfolio equity/fixed income ratio and the annual withdrawal rate in determining how long your money is likely to last during retirement. It also demonstrates the danger of shifting to an overly conservative investment strategy during retirement. If your portfolio can't offset the effects of inflation, you run the

Chart 5.2 WILL YOUR RETIREMENT MONEY LAST?

Do You Feel Lucky?

What are the chances your retirement money will last 30 years?
How much can you reasonably afford to withdraw?

20-Year Retirement	Stock/Bond Portfolio Mix					
Withdrawal rate	100/0	80/20	60/40	40/60	15/85	5/95
4%	97%	99%	100%	100%	100%	100%
5%	91	93	95	96	97	93
6%	76	78	77	70	48	19
7%	56	53	46	28	2	0

25-Year Retirement	Stock/Bond Portfolio Mix					
Withdrawal rate	100/0	80/20	60/40	40/60	15/85	5/95
4%	93%	95%	96%	97%	98%	93%
5%	78	79	79	66	46	14
6%	59	56	48	27	2	0
7%	38	31	18	3	0	0

30-Year Retirement	Stock/Bond Portfolio Mix					
Withdrawal rate	100/0	80/20	60/40	40/60	15/85	5/95
4%	85%	88%	86%	85%	71%	37%
5%	68	66	58	42	8	0
6%	47	41	28	10	0	0
7%	24	18	7	1	0	0

Past performance does not assure future results. Source: T. Rowe Price Associate / WSJ
The market for all securities involves risks, such as loss of principal.

very real risk of going broke before you die. It's vital to have a clear picture of the statistical probabilities of the various asset allocation ratios, the annual rate of withdrawal you plan on and the future purchasing power of your retirement funds.

Tomorrow is an Unknown

When the markets spiral down and the media puts out a steady stream of bad news, investors become alarmed, even frightened. Suddenly they are not worried about double-digit returns; they want safety. They are now ready to listen to advisors preach the virtues of conservative investments. This is especially true of people near to or in retirement. Bad news sells bonds, as they say. Of course, the markets eventually recover and those who pulled out miss out on the rebound, which often includes the best months or year of the decade.

When the markets tanked in 2002, investors ran for cover like deer being chased by lions. The media poured out the doom and gloom: "The financial world is crashing, it may never recover, this time it really is different..." The emotional selling that went on during this period was historic. Then dawned 2003, the best market in three decades! Many who abandoned the markets just months before missed the rebound and never recovered.

The "experts" always tell us what to do based on what happened yesterday, which is almost always the exact opposite of what we should be doing. Financial product producers are smart. They know that severe market movements induce investors to make emotionally charged decisions, so they take advantage of big market swings – up or down – to sell product based on investor reactions to the latest news.

Know this: no one knows what will happen tomorrow. No one. If they did, they would trade on this information, make a fast fortune for themselves, buy one of those yachts they show in their commercials, and sail off into the sunset. But they don't know what will happen tomorrow.

Sometimes they get lucky. When they do, they tell the world how smart they are and investors come running to their door for more wisdom. When they are wrong, they ignore their failures and wait for the next opportunity to sell product based on another prediction.

Avoid the prognosticators. Instead, build an investment strategy that you believe in, that works for your risk tolerance, your needs, your peace of mind, and your financial DNA. Be realistic about who you are and whether your goals are achievable. If they aren't, decide on your course of action. Should you retire with less, retire later, save more now, or make your money work harder?

Make sure you have accurate information and that you are being realistic about your retirement needs and finances. NASA astronauts spend years training and rehearsing for those critical few minutes right before liftoff. They must be absolutely sure there are no miscalculations, mistakes or malfunctions because once they lift off, it's too late to go back and start over. Learn to think of your retirement planning the same way because, if you miscalculate, it's too late to go back and start over once you have retired. Unless, of course, you consider a job as a WalMart greeter at age 75 a post-retirement strategy option. Make sure you have completed your training and checked everything on your pre-flight list before you takeoff for retirement.

Pre-Retirement Risk Tolerance

It's important to have a clear understanding of your portfolio's investment return expectations, including how much those returns are likely to vary. I wince whenever a retiree tells me, "My advisor told me my portfolio should provide an 8% annual return, and then it lost 15% the first year." Often, advisors don't fully explain what an expected annual rate of return really means. Clients interpret it to mean they will receive 8% returns every year, but that's not at all the case. While the portfolio might average around 8% over a period of two or three decades, it is going to have some down years – and some can be significantly down. Losing 15% or more in a given year is not at all unusual, but if the loss comes as a surprise because the advisor did not explain the probability up front, it can feel devastating.

Finding Financial Harmony

One of the most meaningful benefits of having a sound financial plan is that it allows you to enjoy a purposeful retirement. The fuzziness about what you are going to do when you retire is eliminated. A plan will clarify what you want to do and why. It also assures that you have sufficient funds to do the things you want to do. Whatever your goals, if they are realistic you can be more confident knowing that you will be able to do something constructive, something to help others less fortunate and leave a positive imprint on the space you occupied while here.

While statistics show that there is an alarming rise in divorces, substance abuse and suicides during retirement, people with a plan have fewer problems with these issues. They know there will be good days and bad days, but they don't obsess over the bad days because they have a purpose, whether it is to help their family, church, community, charity or a favorite cause. If you plan well prior to retirement, you may be able to contribute even more to your favorite charity during retirement than you did during your working years. It's truly amazing the things you can accomplish and contribute to the world. It's a wonderful uplifting thought to carry into retirement.

By having a transition focus, you can reach your true potential. You can have peace of mind and a rewarding and satisfying late life. Having a plan helps alleviate the fear and chaos that can result in being another regrettable retirement statistic.

As I've mentioned before, money alone won't make you happy, but lack of it will make you unhappy. It's particularly true as you approach retirement because you're running out of time to accumulate money for your late life. If you spend your retirement fretting over every up or down tick of the markets, you will never know peace or experience the joy of contributing to the happiness of others. If you constantly worry about your finances, you give off negative energy that infects those around you. You will never feel the excitement of becoming something bigger than yourself, whether that something is being a better grandparent, neighbor, church member or benefactor. In short, it's difficult to be purposeful in retirement without adequate funds. A solid, long-term plan eliminates that concern.

Making Hard Choices

Retirement planning must be based on a realistic thought process. If what you want to do in retirement doesn't align with where you are, what you have and how hard it is working, you must make some strategic choices. Too often people dread confronting the hard choices and, instead, do nothing, hoping that everything will somehow work out for their retirement. It rarely happens. If the hard choice means you will have to work an extra few years in order to have 25 or 30 years of peace and fulfillment in retirement, that's a smart trade off. But it's not a decision your advisor should make; it must be yours. Your advisor's role is to clarify your options and help you think through them so you can make good choices. It's important that when you step off that working plank, you have a safe place to step onto. Whatever decisions you make will be alright as long as they are based on factual reality and not some rosy fantasy cooked up by a product marketer.

Reality includes having some bad things happen in free markets, so don't fear them; instead, plan for them. Have a strategic process that allows for unforeseen events that are bound to occur. That way, you won't have to expend energy worrying about them. Have a plan so you can deal with probable, yet unexpected outcomes that should be expected. By doing this, you can channel your energy into the excitement and joy of living your life, focusing on the things you really want to do during retirement.

◆◆◆

6

The Retirement Phase

"Lasting confidence and serenity come only
through discovering your purpose for living."
– Wayne von Borstel

It's important to remember that retirement is not an isolated event, but rather one of many events that occur along the journey of life. It is a continuation of the thousands of small decisions we make during our working years, leading up to retirement. Although it is just one more event in our financial continuum, it is the point at which we typically determine what we will have in terms of wealth, happiness and choices for the rest of our life.

No matter what we have or do during retirement, we must find strive for freedom from financial worry. That means not having to worry about money. There is no serenity for people who are consumed with concerns about their money.

Some people get up at the crack of dawn so they can check the markets. They get a rush from the excitement and anxiety the markets produce. But most of my clients prefer the tranquility of being able to ignore the whipsawing of the markets, of not having to worry about what their stocks are doing, especially in the short-term.

Once you reach retirement, you need to be in a state of mind where you have faith in the financial decisions you have made. You need to be confident that you clearly understand your investment strategy and your risk tolerance level. Whatever risk parameters you have chosen, you need to recognize that there will be a certain variance and feel comfortable with it; you shouldn't have to worry about the variance caused by the ups and downs of the markets, nor be surprised when it occurs, because you have built in an acceptable level of variance into your retirement plan.

This means you have met the four criteria, previously mentioned, for successfully moving into retirement:

- You have an emergency fund equal to six months of lifestyle cash flow
- You can live on three percent of your financial assets
- You have five years worth of income in conservative assets
- You have no debt

Securing these four requirements and having complete confidence in your plan, investment strategy and risk tolerance allows you to stop thinking about money.

Instead, you can go fish, golf, garden or play with your grandchildren. If you have adequate resources, you will be able to adjust for most financial or health contingencies that arise. No matter what happens, you'll be better off if you plan than if you don't.

Wealth Can Be Lost

The financial upheaval and prolonged economic downturn that followed the 2008 financial crisis eroded the confidence of many retirees who believed they had more than enough resources to last the rest of their lives. I've spoken to hundreds of people at financial seminars and education classes who lost 50% or more of their retirement savings when the markets collapsed. They had never faced a situation like that in their lifetime, and they didn't know what to do. Whatever they did, it seemed to be wrong.

Even in good times, people unwittingly make poor financial decisions that result in significant loss of wealth. When this occurs after retirement, the options for regaining wealth are severely limited. The result can be both financially and emotionally debilitating.

Consider the couple that retired after selling their fast food franchise for $2.75 million, payable over five years. Enjoying their newfound financial freedom, the couple took a month-long cruise, bought a new Mercedes, refurnished their home, added a greenhouse, and threw an extravagant wedding for a favorite niece ... all in their first two years of retirement.

9 REASONS PEOPLE FAIL FINANCIALLY WHEN PREPARING FOR RETIREMENT

1. Procrastination

2. Don't set clear financial goals

3. Don't have a plan for reaching goals

4. Unwise use of credit

5. Lack of financial education

6. Don't understand and apply tax laws to their advantage

7. Unprepared for the unexpected

8. Don't have an estate plan

9. Don't have a "winning attitude"

After treating their extended family to a Christmas holiday in Hawaii, they realized they had received 40% of their payout and hadn't saved a dime. Their family, understandably, thinks the couple is rich and expectations are they will always have money, so there is enormous temptation for them to continue to spend and enjoy. The couple now realizes they may run out of money and have to start over again in their 60s.

Without a solid retirement plan and an appropriate risk tolerance strategy, wealth that has been accumulated over a lifetime can be depleted or destroyed in a remarkably short time. This is especially true for those who acquire wealth from the sale of a business, an inheritance or other financial windfalls. Even those who merely save a few dollars out of each paycheck over the course of their working lives may find themselves faced with the dilemma of what to do with a large sum of money when they cash in their 401(k).

Retirees at seminars often tell me they have several hundred thousand dollars parked in bank accounts. Because they have seen others lose money by investing in real estate or stocks and, lacking a caring financial coach, they are paralyzed by fear and are afraid to do anything. Instead, they continue earning 1% interest on their taxable money, when they could be earning 4-5%, tax-deferred. If this continues, they can't expect to retain their purchasing power. Inflation and taxes are not going to go away, and for the rest of your life will be competing for your money. However, many retirees feel as though they have been beaten up and knocked down financially and are afraid to play the game anymore. They are standing on the sidelines, waiting until it's safe to go back in; but that's not going to happen. There is no perfect financial situation.

Even in retirement, you have to continue to play the financial game. When you get knocked down, you have to believe you can get up and win the next play. Retirement is not about winning every play, but you must participate if you expect to win the game. If, instead, you choose to sit on the sidelines, you will eventually lose by default. If you try to eliminate market risk with an overly conservative investment strategy, inflation and interest rate risk will defeat you.

Chart 6.1, page 87, shows one aspect of why you have to be in the game. It's important to know what taxes and inflation can do to your goals. If you are in the 25% Federal tax bracket, 10% state tax bracket, and if inflation is 4%, you will only gain 2% puchasing power. For most of us, that is not enough to reach our goals.

The financial media promotes the idea of changing your investment strategy once you retire, not because it is prudent to do so but because they want to sell you product. If you accumulated your retirement assets by investing prudently throughout your working years, there's no reason to change your strategy at age 55 or 60.

Chart 6.1 REAL RATE OF RETURN AFTER TAXES AND INFLATION

Return needed for 2% net return after taxes and inflation[1]		
Inflation Rate	Federal Income Tax bracket		
	15%	25%	35%
2%	4.71%	5.33%	6.15%
3%	5.88%	6.67%	7.69%
4%	7.06%	8.00%	9.23%
5%	8.24%	9.33%	10.76%
6%	9.41%	10.67%	12.31%
7%	10.59%	12.00%	13.85%
8%	11.76%	13.33%	15.38%

1 Investment made and inflation on investment is calculated from the beginning of the year.

Often, people get to retirement and fail financially because they lack a solid plan. They assumed it would all work out … somehow. But, of course, it didn't. A fellow came to my office who had earned a substantial income during his working years. Managing his own portfolio, he had spent three decades chasing returns, bouncing from one investment strategy to another every few years. He was convinced there was a way to consistently earn 25-30% annual returns, and he was determined to find it. However he never did. And now, in his late 50s, his portfolio has deteriorated to the point that he has to earn 30% annual returns just to make his retirement projections work. He left my office disappointed that I had no magic formula to offer him, and I never heard from him again. As far as I know, he is still chasing the impossible.

This fellow didn't want to restrict his spending habits and live an affordable lifestyle. Instead, he wanted to delude himself that there is some secret formula for living without a budget and still having enough for retirement. People do it all the time. Similarly, every day I wake up and think I'm going to weigh a pound less next week. And next week I think the same thing, but I still weigh the same. Without a plan it will never happen. Often, the biggest lies we ever tell are the ones we tell ourselves.

If you have accumulated significant wealth don't think you are immune to losing your money. Consider how many other wealthy people have lost much or all of their money chasing returns, believing a story that is too good to be true, or making emotional investment decisions. How many athletes and celebrities have lost fortunes because they took the advice of someone who told them what they wanted to hear? How many people lost major chunks of their retirement portfolios because they thought real estate could only go one direction? How many eviscerated their portfolios by day trading or following the stock recommendations of some Wall Street talking head?

You need a competent, caring coach to help you make informed decisions, preserve your investment capital and avoid unnecessary risk. No matter how smart or successful, no matter how you accumulated your wealth, you need a shepherd to help you keep your focus on the horizon so you won't be thrown overboard when the next financial storm occurs.

Chart 6.2 RETIREMENT DECISION TREE

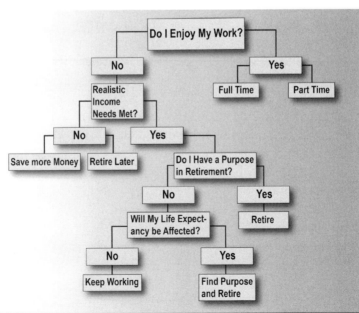

© von Borstel & Associates

What Are You Worth?

When first meeting with prospective clients, I ask them what their net worth is. Seldom do they even come close to an accurate figure. Either they have no idea because no one has sat down with them to determine exactly what they are worth, or they grossly underestimate their net worth. This may surprise you, but in my experience most people simply don't know how much they are worth.

They usually have no idea where they are on the road to retirement nor any concept of how much money they will need over the long term, yet most assume they will have enough … one way or another. Their investment broker or 401(k) specialist may have supported their assumption, but didn't look at their total financial picture. No one has taken the time to create a statistically realistic plan, based on proven academics, that illustrates what needs to be done to ensure they don't run out of money, regardless of the variables that occur.

Everyone needs a plan that is strong enough to withstand the three things we know will happen: the markets will go down, inflation will go up and our health will go sideways. There must be a plan that ensures no matter how, when or how often those three things happen, there will still be a high probability of success. Very few people have undergone that kind of detailed analysis with their financial advisor. Instead, they get their advice from a financial cowboy who wants to herd them into a prepared corral with the lure of free financial advice, advice that invariably leads to the sale of a financial product. What they really need is a financial shepherd who will take care of them and provide unbiased information from the perspective of their individual retirement needs and wishes.

It saddens me to see people buy into the idea of free advice or a free financial plan when we all know nothing worthwhile is free. The same applies to the perception that "cheap" is good. Those who are brainwashed into believing cheap is better are gambling their financial futures.

A Collapsing Nest

The economic downturn that began in 2008 has forced many young and not-so-young adults to move back in with their parents. While not necessarily a bad thing in terms of keeping family generations together, adult children moving back home can imperil retirement plans. Problems occur when parents fail to hold their live-in children accountable for supporting themselves, a kindness that can be detrimental to the children ever accepting personal responsibility.

Regardless of the economic environment, children must go to work and become self-sufficient. I have seen instances where parental benevolence facilitates children becoming permanently dependent. Future generations are damaged or destroyed when parents unintentionally enable children to become members of a welfare society. Once the parents die, the children are unable to support themselves and, quite possibly with children of their own, are helpless. Children must be weaned for their benefit, as well as that of their parents. Cows wean their calves so they learn to eat and digest food on their own and become healthy adults. It's natural and good for both the cow and her calves. Without weaning, the next generation of calves would be weak and unable to survive.

Parents who fail to shove their children out the door to find work and become productive citizens are leaving a legacy of sloth that cannot survive. The longer the tolerance continues, the more trapped the parents become. After a certain period of time, it becomes emotionally and physically impossible for parents to push their birds out of the nest and force them to fly. It's such a frightening prospect for the children that they simply refuse to do it. Many of these children do not comprehend the price their parents paid in order to be financially sound in retirement. The concept of working two jobs, living on a budget and saving for the future is completely foreign to them. Many children and young adults today believe they are *entitled* to everything their parents worked so hard to acquire, and even more. They were never forced to sacrifice or to do without. Perhaps the reason roughly 70% of adults in the U.S. reach retirement with literally no savings is because they believe merely being born in this country entitles them to a life of fulfillment without earning it.

I know people in their seventies who are not achieving their financial goals because they have children who are still dependent on them and are unable to function as financial entities. So talk to your kids about money and what it means, and what saving and debt-free means. Try to instill in them a work ethic and a sense of pride in what they do and what they become. Your life and theirs will be the better for it. I believe the country will be better for it. In addition, you will likely never have to worry about them moving back in with you once you are retired.

Finding Contentment

It's always difficult to advise a client they shouldn't do something or buy something they want. It doesn't feel good for the client or me, but when it is in their best interest, I am obliged ... whether pleasant or not. Even wealthy people have limitations and are better off learning to be satisfied with what they have. Just because someone can afford to buy a condo in Hawaii doesn't mean it's a good idea. They may experience temporary pleasure, but as that feeling fades they soon feel the need to buy something else, something grander and likely more expensive. They are once again chasing happiness by acquiring something new.

Although Wall Street and corporate America's marketing blitz may be what keeps the economy humming and growing, to be successful as individuals, we have to put a governor on our urges, set realistic goals and agree to be happy with what we have. If we are not happy today, when will we be happy? There will always be people with more money, bigger homes, a grander lifestyle, and if money and possessions are what drive you, if that becomes your legacy, you will never be truly happy.

A famous psychologist once said, "Happiness is largely a matter of getting rid of the things in your life that cause you stress." For years, I had two magnificent saltwater fish tanks in my office. My schedule required I delegate care of the tanks to others who didn't care as much about the fish as I did. We had a few disasters, and worrying about the fish caused me enormous stress. I loved those fish but it was best for me to get rid of them. I'm sad they are gone, but I needed to do it. I will have less stress over the long term and will be happier.

Leaving a Footprint

One benefit of growing up on the farm was that I quickly realized life was not perfect. I learned about disability and death because it happened with regularity. Like farm animals, humans get sick, have accidents and die. It's all part of everyday life. As humans, the better we plan, the more contingencies we cover, the more likely we are to survive natural events we can't control.

At age 30, I lost everything. I decided I would leave the farm to build a career in the financial services industry and try to make the best use of the skills I possessed. I hired various types of coaches over the ensuing years to help me become better. It all helped, and while I may or may not have reached my maximum potential, I know I have come close. As a result, I have enjoyed remarkable success and I am now able to give back. Even though I gave up a lot, making sacrifices in spending and time along the way, I feel fortunate to be born in the USA and have the opportunity to reach the point where I am.

Many people never get that opportunity; they never get to make that choice. I plan to give back each year by helping to build a school somewhere in the world where it's needed, a place where they don't have hope. By doing this, if I live another 30 years I will have built 30 schools. In spite of governments, catastrophes and unforeseen events that may erode my efforts, if just half of them survive I will have provided opportunities for thousands of children. And, if just a small percentage of them have their lives changed for the better, it's well worth the effort. By affecting how they think and make decisions, a better world has been created for them.

Often, people are so busy accumulating things and worrying about unimportant things, they never think about how they can maximize their potential in the world. Or they may think they don't have enough time or enough money to contribute. Yet even the simplest gesture can make a big difference.

I'm reminded of Charlie Davis, a farmer I worked for many years ago. He never attended college and went bankrupt three times. He lived in a shack, wore bib overalls and drove a 35-year-old car. When Charlie died at the age of 85, he left a significant amount of money to a local high school. My nephew, who was not even born when Charlie was alive, recently graduated from that school. He and every other graduate was the beneficiary of a gift from a man they had never met. Each got a gift from Charlie Davis, a man who lived in a shack.

Charlie has left a footprint that goes beyond the grave. Most of us die and our great-great grandkids won't even know our names. Yet, we can all leave a footprint. We can effect real and enduring change. Those of us who have been blessed with significant wealth have the rare opportunity to leave a meaningful footprint.

Finding Your Purpose

Serenity comes from having a purpose in life – beyond that of making money and acquiring possessions. Allowing money to be your driving force will invariably lead to chaos. Lasting confidence and serenity come only through discovering your purpose for living.

People who have a purpose have longer life expectancies. Your purpose can be linked to your love of a sport or activity – fishing or golf, for example. It can also be a higher purpose, such as protecting the environment or charitable work. The choice is less important than having a purpose in itself.

Many retirees prefer to continue working because they enjoy it, not because they need the money. Working is a fulfilling part of their social lives. For some, work serves the same purpose as a hobby. If you enjoy your work, but do not have to work in order to fulfill your needs, you might consider working on a part-time or pro bono basis.

Of course, another reason to have a purpose is that your spouse may not be ready or willing to deal with you 24/7. If you are not going to work anymore, you need to find something on which to focus your energy.

Love Letters and Recordings

For many years I searched for a way to get to know my clients better, so I could do a better job of being their advocate. I hit upon the idea of having my clients pretend they had just died and would never get to talk to their loved ones again. I asked them to write a letter to their spouses, children or anyone they loved and cared about, telling them the things they wished they had expressed while they were alive. The letters expressed their love, the special times and cherished memories they shared, and what they had planned for the future. I wanted them to see what was truly important. I also felt these letters would become treasured family heirlooms, passed down and read by future generations.

Some of my clients did indeed write the letters and expressed thanks for urging them to do so. However, many chose not to do it. I have overcome the resistance of most of them by suggesting they, instead, allow me to record a conversation with them each year for three or four years. As a facilitator during these sessions, I ask a few questions to get the conversation rolling and then recede into the background. I encourage them to talk about their personal history, where they grew up and what their life was like as a child. What did they learn from their parents and grandparents? What was their first job, their first recollection about money? What does money mean to them now? What do they worry about? What is their wish for the money they leave behind?

I ask them to talk about the people who made the greatest impression on them, who were the most significant people in their life? Who was most responsible for them becoming who they are?

What were the most important or interesting events in their life? What do they value most? What formed their value system? What turned out to be the most important lesson they learned? What wisdom do they want to pass on to those left behind?

The results have been heartwarming and productive. Clients recall events they haven't thought about in years, often with an emotional reaction. They remember things they intended to say to their loved ones that were somehow forgotten. They talk about their plans for the future and their hopes for their children. They explain their decisions in raising their offspring and how they tried to pass on their values. They talk about the meaningful events that formed their values, the choices they made early in life, the paths they took and those they didn't.

A client who had been rather guarded about sharing information opened up during her taping. A native Alaskan, she recalled how her parents and eight siblings were forcibly huddled into a resettlement camp by the government during WWII. They endured a hardscrabble existence, subsisting on meager rations of lard and little more for several years. Her mother became ill and died while there, and she harbors some understandably bitter and unforgiving feelings about the experience.

Had she not shared that experience, I would never have understood the motivations behind her financial decisions and would certainly have been a far less effective advocate for her.

I recall another woman who had remained virtually silent over the years during the many meetings I had with her and her husband. She initially struck me as a bit eccentric, until she began to divulge her history in our first recorded conversation.

In painful detail, she described how her mother, born in England, had been sent to a concentration camp during WWII. Her father, a native Italian, was conscripted into the war and not permitted to see his wife. My client was only four years of age and her sister six when they were permanently separated from their parents. The two girls were supposed to be sent to another country, but a family maid refused to abandon the girls and stayed on to raise them, despite the family's home being in a war zone in Italy. They survived on the front lines with virtually nothing. When the Allies invaded, the three hid in the woods outside the home as bullets flew overhead during gunfire exchanges with the German and Italian forces.

After hearing those haunting tales of her childhood, I gained a much better understanding of how she felt about her home, security, money and other issues. Because of her personal history, she cannot think about the world in the same manner I do, but after hearing her amazing survival story, her attitudes seemed perfectly natural and not at all eccentric.

These conversations have a remarkable ability to take people to a place of safety where they can open doors to their history. Client privilege precludes me from sharing their gratitude, but I can tell you that if all of this had never resulted in a dollar of additional income, it still would have been an enlightening activity for my clients, my professional practice and for me personally. It has created a glow that I carry with me every day.

As a result of these tapings, I understand my clients' motivations and thinking better. While we might not agree on a particular strategy or order of priority, this becomes relatively unimportant within the context of having this newly formed connection. We can disagree yet still get along and make important planning progress because I know them so much better.

I wish I could listen to my great-grandparents tell me about their amazing lives. I've gone back to their birthplace in Germany. I stared at the beautiful, lush green farmland they left to come to America and I have wondered why they settled on the barren, sagebrush-strewn farmland in Oregon. The two settings are so dramatically different; I'm at a loss why they chose this place as their new home. How did they survive the first three brutally cold winters living in a tent while nearly all their neighbors either perished or abandoned farming? I want to know these things but can't.

As I conduct the recordings for my clients and for their future generations, I know I am doing something worthwhile. One of my clients is a pastor and the best sermon on money I've ever heard was not delivered from a pulpit on a Sunday morning but rather from my pastor sitting alone with me during his first conversation.

No matter how much money you leave, it will someday be worthless if you fail to leave some useful knowledge with it. Teaching your children and grandchildren what you have learned regarding money, success and being happy with what you have is worth far more than any amount of money you might leave behind. Money frequently gets wasted; knowledge will last for a lifetime and, hopefully, be passed on to the following generation.

While all of your knowledge and understanding in different areas may not be significant, some of it will be. The knowledge you have accumulated may be more important to your future generations than anything they will learn from books written by historians.

Some who listen to what you have to say will laugh and ignore it, but others will listen and learn the reasons for who they are, where they came from and why. Those are the ones who will take your knowledge and create a better future. I know people with family wealth who have no idea where it originated. If you leave a good letter or recording, it will likely be in your family one hundred years from now. By then, no one will remember how much wealth you left behind, but from your conversations, they will know what kind of person you were, what you valued, and that you cared enough to pass on the knowledge you gained during your lifetime. And they will profit from it.

Summary

My grandma was my biggest inspiration. She's been dead for 15 years, but I vowed to never do anything to embarrass her. She believed in me and was proud of me even when I hadn't given her much reason to be proud. She taught me to care about people and I'm a better planner today because of what she taught me. She also taught me to have a positive attitude.

I'm not the most handsome guy. I went deaf at 49, have a bad back and have to get medical treatment twice a year so I can walk. But I think life is great. I can't smell or taste, but life is still good because I recognize how lucky I am in other, more important areas. I could get depressed and say life is not fair and play the role of victim, but all that would accomplish is to force me into making losing choices and not a very pleasant person to be around. We can't control all the bad that happens merely by being positive, but life will be better for us if we control our attitude.

If we give off negative energy and money is the ultimate goal, we will have a negative life. If we are positive and understand that money is merely a tool in the pursuit of happiness, we are much more likely to have a happy life.

I appreciate what I have, and I play to win with what I have because no matter what happens, I know I will be better off for living this way. I hope this book encourages you to do the same.

◆◆◆

7

Estate Planning

"If you are no longer around, who will be your
children's advocate? Who will tell them what
they need to know about money when they
don't want to hear it?"

– Wayne von Borstel

During their working years, most people view estate planning as mainly making sure they have sufficient life insurance. They buy tomorrows for their beneficiaries in case they don't have enough time to build an estate.

Previously I mentioned how our second child, Nicholas, lived for just one short month. His medical bills were such that without insurance my wife and I would not have the lives we do today. I don't think God intended bad things to happen to us but, if we hadn't done the right thing regarding insurance, our lives would have been a financial disaster. Perhaps I could have negotiated payments with the hospital, the three surgeons, the anesthetist and the ambulance services, but I would have owed those people forever. We could have been sucked into a financial black hole and never got out.

Most people don't understand or like to think about what can happen to them. No one would have predicted that Nicholas, who seemed so healthy when he was born, would die 30 days later from an unidentified cause. But, suddenly he was gone and only the bills remained. However, because we planned in advance we were able to survive financially. The loss of our child created a permanent hole in our lives, and I still cry when I think about him and what happened; but our lives didn't end.

Growing up on the farm gave me the strength and understanding that death is a natural part of life. Bad things happen; they aren't anyone's fault. They just happen. But you can never assume you are immune to them. Twice I fell off horses and I don't know why I didn't die either of those days. You must protect your family and yourself so you don't lose everything when these things happen.

During your working years, it's essential to buy life insurance and have an estate plan. Hopefully, you will be lucky and live a long, healthy life and everything will be perfect, but God provides us with no guarantees. Make sure you have adequate life insurance and an estate plan to ensure the people you love will be okay in case you are not there to take care of them.

Power of Attorney

One day my wife received a phone call from a hospital in nearby Corvallis. Our daughter, who was attending college there, had been hit by a car and was in the hospital. The land speed record my wife broke getting there would have been for naught had we not had our daughter complete and sign medical and financial Powers of Attorney (POA) before leaving for college. Without them, no one could have talked to us about her treatment – not the doctors, her employer, or anyone at Oregon State University. The day your child is injured is not the day you want to discover that you need these documents.

This is why it is critical that every family member, 18 years or older, have POAs for both financial and medical directions. If, like us, your son or daughter has an automobile accident and is hospitalized, this is the only way you will be able to make decisions about the treatment. And, with a financial POA, you will be able to make vital financial decisions for injured or impaired children, decisions that will determine the conditions in which they may have to live for decades.

In some respects, the financial POA may be even more critical than a medical one. While medical issues may be huge, the medical community will do it's best to keep them alive and to see them through to recovery, even though it may not be the way you or your children would have preferred. On the other hand, the financial community will not take care of them. For example, if someone is seriously injured to the extent they are in a coma for an extended period of time, they may recover only to find their home and all their possessions have been taken away. Financial lives are turned upside-down, while courts struggle and families suffer. What quality of life does this afford them?

Once your children turn 18, make certain you have these two legal documents completed, signed and always available. This also applies to all the adults in your family. And, in case of a sudden illness or accident, make sure someone you love can take care of, and make decisions for you.

AUTHOR'S NOTE: *Because medical directives are state-specific, if you live in one state but your children attend school in another, it's advisable to have medical POAs for both states. For adults, if you have homes in two different states or spend a significant amount of time in another state, it's also appropriate to have separate medical POAs for each state.*

Beneficiaries

I have never attended a funeral where people talked about the investment returns of the deceased. However, I have heard many funeral conversations asking why the deceased didn't have a will, life insurance, proper documents, or why they didn't put more aside for the family left behind. Planning is about people, pure and simple. And, at the end of day, it protects those we care most about.

During every phase of your life, it's imperative that you keep these documents updated and that you name and update the designated beneficiaries on your insurance policies, 401(k), IRA and annuities. As people go through life, they often fail to notice the changes that occur. Priorities change, and the people they care about can change. They think differently, have children, establish businesses, grow assets, and gain new partners or spouses. Although things change, people often neglect to change their beneficiaries in response to them. People who are ill and dying may know their beneficiaries are wrong, yet they still don't do anything about it. Perhaps they think they won't die as soon if they don't make the changes. I've seen it happen with regularity and I am powerless to do anything about it if people won't act.

In my experience, there are usually more things wrong than right with beneficiaries. For example, most people list their spouse as first beneficiary on their 401(k). Years later, as they approach the end of their accumulation stage, their 401(k) may be their largest asset, aside from their home. However, they never took the time to name a second beneficiary. When they die, the second beneficiary is often the most important one because the first beneficiary may have died previously or at the same time, such as in the case of an accident. Or sometimes the spouse named as first beneficiary is no longer the spouse.

It's very frustrating to see the consequences of having the wrong beneficiaries listed.

Following are some examples of situations I've seen and the problems that were created:

Case Study #1

A woman I know spent six months attending to her dying husband. She gave up her career to nurse him through his final months of life. After his death, a friend suggested she ask me to help her sort out his insurance and estate. It took a couple of weeks to secure and review all his documents and, to her horror, we discovered his first wife's children were the beneficiaries of everything he owned. During his last days, he had repeatedly told her how much he loved her, appreciated what she was doing for him and that he had made her beneficiary on his policies and investment portfolio. I'm sure he was sincere; he probably thought he had made the changes but, for whatever reason, he had not. The poor woman had given up everything to help him during his last days and ended up with nothing.

Case Study #2

When I was a young man selling life insurance, I called on a couple who owned a dry cleaning shop. He had purchased a life policy prior to their marriage, and I suggested we spend a few minutes reviewing it. The husband agreed, but said he was too busy that day and asked me to call him in a couple of months. Before I could do that, his wife called to say he had died suddenly, and she and her two-year-old daughter were desperate for money so they could remain in their home. When we reviewed the policy, we found his beneficiary was two wives removed. His current wife was frantic, but there was nothing I could do for her.

Case Study #3

One day a young woman came to see me. Her husband had recently been killed in an industrial accident. Her mother, a client of mine, suggested that she seek my help in getting insurance reimbursement. We went through the discovery process, complicated by the lawsuits associated with the accident. When we were finally able to inspect the husband's documents, what we found was sad, but not unusual. He had started his job 15 years earlier when their only child at that time was a two year-old daughter. However, by the time of his death, they had two more children.

When we put in the claim for benefits, we learned that when the husband originally filled out the life insurance form, he listed his wife on the first line and his oldest child, a now 17-year-old daughter, on the second, thinking the lines represented first and second beneficiary. But they did not; they represented co-beneficiaries. This meant his wife was only entitled to half of the benefits and the other half went to the oldest daughter, who was now an out-of-control teenager with a drug habit. Meanwhile, the other two children were disinherited. Again, there was little I could do for this poor woman and her other two children.

Case Study #4

Early in my career, I had many farmers as clients. These farm families often had little money but great land wealth. For them, relationship-oriented solutions had to go beyond merely getting the numbers right. It was important to create estate plans that would not break up the family. One farmer who never got along with his siblings insisted the only fair treatment for his five children was to make them equal beneficiaries of the family farm. Today, only one of his kids works the farm. Two are in financial trouble. The fourth has no interest in what happens to the farm, and the fifth is a successful physician who doesn't need the farm's income. What's the likelihood these children will remain friendly?

An estate plan where the heirs all receive an equal share of the assets can be a huge miscalculation, good intentions notwithstanding. I've seen situations where poor planning creates disharmony, mistrust, legal action and even fisticuffs among family members. If there is the slightest risk that the plan can result in family members never talking to one another again, it's time to go back to square one and find a better solution. No asset is worth destroying a family. Fair, equitable and equal don't always mean the same thing.

Case Study #5

A few years ago, a woman asked me to talk to her husband about their estate. For years she had been trying to get him to sit down with an advisor and go over everything to see if any changes were necessary. After reviewing the couple's financial documents, I suggested the husband take advantage of a one-time opportunity that year to pay zero estate taxes. The potential savings were significant, given their estate was in excess of $40 million. He said he would think it over, but died a few weeks later without doing anything. Because he procrastinated, his wife wound up with just a few million and his two children received virtually nothing. Most of the money went to the government.

Here was a highly intelligent entrepreneur who was phenomenally successful at accumulating money. He had the vision to build and grow wealth, but didn't have the vision to get help to retain and transfer it to the next generation. It was a terrible tragedy that could have been avoided, but he was sure no one would care as much about his money as he did. He was confident that he didn't need a financial coach to help him do what was best for him and his family.

After he died, his wife told me his health had been declining for several years. Isn't it amazing? Even when someone knows they are dying, they don't believe death will ever actually come. People must subconsciously believe they are not really going to die, so they fail to do anything to ensure their documents are correct. Instead, they commit financial suicide.

Being involved in a business can have its own set of problems. For example, the original buy/sell agreement is unlikely to mesh with the owner's financial or estate plan if the business falters, the owner acquires a new business partner or becomes successful in another business.

As businesses evolve so do the lives of the principals. Partnership agreements change, real estate is bought and sold, investors die. As circumstances change, existing documents and agreements may no longer accurately reflect a person's interests or wishes, creating a convoluted mess. Unfortunately, no one takes the time to see how all the various legal documents were supposed to work together.

An estate plan is like having farm equipment. From time to time you have to replace worn parts with new ones from various manufacturers to keep the machinery working well. Similarly, someone has to keep an eye on all the ingredients of a person's financial life as time goes by to make sure everything runs well … that it meshes. These horror stories are the reason why you must check your beneficiary designations on a regular basis. There is a good chance you will find that they no longer accurately represent your intentions.

Documents and Intentions

I've examined more than 600 estate plans in my career and have yet to see one that reflects the exact wishes of the owner. That's an amazing statistic, but it's true. When I compare the beneficiaries, ownership of assets and documents with the intentions of the owner, they almost never match. There is usually an inaccuracy, misunderstanding or conflict.

Often, no one helps them go through the estate plan discovery process until there is a death, and by then it's too late to make corrections. Many people have told me they were confident everything in their plan was accurate and their beneficiaries were correct because they had an attorney draft the documents. Unfortunately, attorneys get paid to prepare documents as instructed by their clients, not to analyze motivations or objectives. Most attorneys do a thoughtful and competent job, but they are not in the business of questioning how the various elements might or might not work together. That's why it is important to get a second opinion. Unfortunately, most people don't want to pay someone to perform this kind of analysis, yet it is critically important. If you are reading this and saying to yourself, "I know my estate plan is completely accurate and reflects my wishes," I strongly suggest you reconsider having a knowledgeable professional review your plan. In my experience, the odds are six hundred to zero that there are, hidden in the complexity of your document, inappropriate results not aligned with your current wishes, or the lack thereof.

It's important to select a dedicated attorney who specializes in estate planning. Estate planning calls for anticipating the unanticipated, making provisions for things we can't envision happening, and it must work regardless of what happens in the future or what circumstances exist when the owner dies. Your advisor and attorney have to be sufficiently competent to create a plan with the flexibility to adjust to whatever happens.

Most people choose an attorney by asking a friend or associate for a recommendation. The role of an estate planning attorney is too important to choose one casually or to follow the recommendation of someone who really doesn't know whether their attorney has done a competent job for them, because they aren't dead yet. I believe most attorneys are honest and try to do a good job. However, they frustrate me when it comes to estate planning.

Attorneys recognize that the complexities of estate planning often confuse clients and so they tend to dumb down the conversations to avoid prolonged discussions that may deter clients from moving forward with the documents. They also know the less detail they go into, the fewer problems they will have to deal with, hence less work.

In discussions with attorneys chosen by clients, I often find them unreceptive to any ideas the clients may have that are at all unusual or creative. They prefer to keep things simple and follow a template. Often, they don't even listen to what the client wants if it falls outside the attorney's established parameters or personal preferences for documentation. Clients can easily be intimidated during the estate planning process and succumb to their attorney's desire to do things a certain way. After all, there's no way for clients to know what they don't know. A plan that is easier for the attorney to execute may be fundamentally sound yet not fulfill what is most important to the client.

Some attorneys routinely prescribe advice that is more focused on their own interests and convenience than that of their clients. Others may actually see it as an opportunity to earn more money. After all, if beneficiaries fight because the way estate documents are set up, more legal fees ensue. That's a harsh statement but it happens to be a fact of life in our legal system.

Clients need someone to take the time to explore their true wishes, what they want their documents to accomplish, who and how the beneficiaries should be assigned, how their assets should be owned, and whether all those considerations match up. Estate plans should be very specific and personal, not something created from a template or a generic plan that works for most people. Each of us has his or her own financial DNA; our estate plan should reflect that DNA and align it with our wishes.

Here's something few people think about when creating an estate plan: Everything you have accumulated, learned and care about should be passed on to your next generation or the organizations you wish to help. Your estate plan should reflect your dreams for the future, not the assumptions of an attorney who hardly knows you. Isn't it important to you that the culmination of your lifetime, the knowledge and wealth you created be used as you intended?

Estate Planning Principles

There is a set of four principles I apply when helping clients create their estate plan, rules that help prevent battles between beneficiaries over estate assets. While not terribly complex or difficult to follow, they are frequently broken by the unwary and by attorneys whose primary concern is not maintaining family harmony.

Forgive me for breaking the adage of never saying "never" but I'm going to break that rule in order to emphasize the importance of adhering to these fundamental principles.

PRINCIPLE #1: Never name co-executors or co-trustees.

> One person should be designated as executor or trustee, another as alternate. If the estate plan names co-trustees or co-executors and they disagree on anything, they may be fighting for the rest of their lives. While parents may not want any of their offspring to become upset as a result of not being designated first, a child who is going to be upset because a sibling was named probably shouldn't be trustee or executor in the first place.

Beneficiaries often become emotional warriors the day they inherit money. It's hard to predict how they will act toward one another once money is involved. If there's no decision maker, they will go to war. I know of a case where two sisters never talked to each other again because of a fight over a ten-dollar teapot that had sentimental value. Two other siblings spent $20,000 in litigation over a coffee table that was virtually worthless, each insisting their mother had promised them the table.

Every estate plan should designate a decision maker. Many parents are incapable of naming one over another because they don't want to show favoritism, even though their wishes won't be known until after they are deceased. The kids will be standing over the coffin when they find out they aren't the trustee; how angry can they be with a dead parent? In any case, they'll get over it.

PRINCIPLE #2: Never put children's names on their parent's assets, or vice versa.

An example is the loving son who took care of his invalid mother while trying to run his nearby farm for a decade. His two siblings lived several hours away and rarely visited or called the elderly woman. The frugal mother, who lived on virtually nothing, had almost $600,000 in savings. She decided to put her caring son's name on her assets to make things easier when she died and because she loved and trusted him.

It wouldn't have taken much rationalization for the son to keep most or all of the inheritance, given his decade-long caretaker sacrifice and the indifference of his siblings. But being an honest fellow, he decided to share the money equally. The problem, of course, was that unless the siblings wanted to inherit some serious gift tax issues along with the money, they were limited to receiving $13,000 a year. So it was going to take almost 15 years for them to get their full shares. Not only did they have to wait, they had no say in how the funds were managed.

Here's another reason not to have children's names on parent's assets. Suppose the mother doesn't die, but one rainy evening the son is driving home and runs over and kills a pedestrian. His mother is still alive, but because he is named on her assets, she is likely to lose half of them.

Similarly, she could lose much of her money if the son is divorced. Ditto if one of his farmhand helpers falls off a tractor and is crippled. Anything that goes wrong in the son's life — divorce, lawsuit, accident, bankruptcy — imperils half of her remaining money. And how well does an 80-year-old widow sleep once she's lost half her money, even if she didn't need it?

I regularly tell clients they should never give their money to their kids unless they're willing to have them nuke it. This goes for personal possessions as well, such as a home or business. I've seen people drive five miles out of their way every time they go to town because they can't stand to drive past the house they gave their kids. They don't like the way it's painted, the grass being three feet tall or the unrepaired fence.

A lot of people give assets away to their kids, expecting them back if they get into financial trouble. I know an 84-year-old man who was living on a ranch in the same house his grandparents had built, and he was born in. Fearing he would lose the ranch if he had to go into long-term care, he gave it to his son. Unfortunately, his son was married to a woman who was a spendthrift. One day the son tells his father it would be best for the old man to move out of the house and into town. It had nothing to do with what was best for him; the son was about to lose the ranch. The old man had to move away from the family farm where he had lived all of his life.

There are times clients should give away assets, but be aware that children sometimes get into financial trouble or divorced.

PRINCIPLE #3: Never leave undivided real property to joint beneficiaries.

My grandfather had six kids. He gave each a section of his farm, hoping they would work the farm together. But they couldn't do it because they were all as different as night and day.

Estate planning is a little like farming. There are always going to be some areas of the farm where you simply can't raise a crop. The only thing those acres are good for is pastureland, and some aren't even suitable for that. When you evaluate your acreage, you need to accept that fact, and decide where you can plant and what crop is best to grow there this year. And what you do this year may not be best next year; corn may do well this year but you may need to rotate and plant wheat next year for the best yield.

Children are the same way; they're all different. Some kids need a different crop. Giving the same to all six of your kids is like treating every area of a farm the same way, regardless of the soil, drainage, rock content or what crop was planted last year. It just isn't the best way. Heirs from future generations will be futher removed from the asset source and will have fewer reasons for getting along.

PRINCIPLE #4: Introduce your children to their financial advocate.

Near where I live in Oregon, we have a lot of winding roads and even more deer. The last time I hit one, I'm pretty sure the deer was having a perfectly wonderful time right up until the moment I came around the bend and broadsided it. That's how it is with children sometimes. We give them all kinds of things because we love them and want them to enjoy themselves. Too often, they wind up like deer, aimlessly wandering about, unaware of the dangers lurking around the next bend. We buy them a sporty car because they beg us for it and we can afford it, then we send them off to play on the highway and expect they will be safe. Or we leave them money with no instructions, and they don't know how to manage or save it.

If you are no longer around, who will be your children's advocate? Who will tell them what they need to know about money when they don't want to hear it? Even smart, successful parents often find it almost impossible to have these discussions because they are such emotional issues.

I try to train the young children of my clients about money, to give them some basic rules and help shape their ideas about wealth. It was Andrew Carnegie who spoke about families going from shirtsleeves and back again in three generations. The first generation earns it, the second tries to deal with it and the third falls so far short of the skill set it took to create it that they cannot preserve it, and so the money is gone before the fourth generation can benefit from it.

If you have a trusted financial advisor, he or she can help prevent generational tragedies and hopefully instill in your children the desire to leave something of importance behind. Advisors shouldn't be expected to be substitute parents, but in a good professional relationship, your advisor knows as much about you, your financial history and your wishes for your children as anyone else. Your advisor can also be your children's confidant, a third party they can trust and talk to about whatever interests or concerns they have.

Your advisor can be a facilitator, someone who can help pass your assets and values to the next generation. I suggest multi-generational meetings with your advisor and your children, so they can get to know each other and establish a trusting relationship. Hopefully this can occur long before you are no longer here to help them.

If you follow these four principles there's a good chance your family members won't be fighting, or worse, in litigation someday.

A Promise

A middle-aged client of mine was diagnosed with an incurable disease. His estate plan contained a life insurance policy that had been written several years before I started working with him. I repeatedly asked to review his plan. However, he told me everything was in order and insisted there was no need to confirm what he already knew. A few weeks before he died, he told his son that he was the sole beneficiary of the life insurance policy, and that he expected the son to use the proceeds to take care of his sister who had special needs and was unable to make her own financial or medical decisions. After the man died, his son discovered the beneficiary was actually his father's first wife, who had an adversarial relationship with the daughter and felt no obligation to her.

Had I been given the opportunity to review that policy, I could have ensured the father's desire to take care of his daughter would be carried out. To this day, I regret not insisting he let me have a look at that paperwork. People can be absolutely sure of something and still be wrong.

Never again do I want to be in a position of not knowing whether my clients' assets and beneficiaries are listed correctly and whether the supporting documents say what the deceased intended. Instead, I want to know I tried the best I could to make sure things were right. If I did my best and they still insist on vetoing the changes I suggest, I can't control the outcome. However, I can decline to work with clients who are not committed to doing their best with their planning process. I don't want to learn that their estate plans are incorrect or incomplete the day of their funerals.

◆◆◆

AUTHOR'S NOTE: *The stories in this chapter are not intended to be a substitue for specific individualized legal advice. Instead, we suggest you discuss your specific situation with a qualified legal advisor.*

8

Why I Do What I Do

"It's important that you find someone you can trust
enough to let him or her in and really know who
you are, what you treasure and what you fear. "
– Wayne von Borstel

A lot of people have brilliant careers yet are surprisingly naïve about money. Even successful or
famous people, who earn an enormous amount of
money, can be lost at sea when it comes to managing their money. Only a small percentage of these
people are coachable. Most believe they can succeed
financially without help, perhaps because of their
professional success. They would rather do things
their own way, and typically have a convincing ra-
tionale as to why they should. Unfortunately, many
of them fail.

Uncoachable people are usually in attendance at
my educational seminars. They listen to my ideas,
sometimes we have a brief conversation afterward
and they may ask a few questions; yet I know they
are going to leave and continue to do things their

own way. While I may think they are making a mistake, I also know they will resist any help I offer because, like the majority of people who think they are above-average drivers, these people genuinely believe they are smart enough to handle their own financial planning and come out winners.

I recall speaking to a renowned vascular surgeon who insisted he could outsmart the markets in his spare time. He seriously believed that by studying some charts a few hours a week, he could beat the professionals who manage money for a living. I knew that nothing I could say would change his mind. However, if that surgeon needs an ankle operation, he's unlikely to tackle this relatively simple procedure himself. Even though all ankles are pretty much the same, and anyone can open a medical textbook, learn about the various bones involved and read how to perform the procedure, he would never think of operating on his own. However, he is willing to tackle the far more complicated task of creating and managing a personalized financial plan.

On the other hand, I know how to manage money, but if I need an ankle operation I want the best doctor I can find. I want one who has performed hundreds or thousands of ankle operations, not someone who is going to use me for practice, or someone who barely made it through med school. It's unfortunate that people don't regard the complicated task of financial planning the same way they do their medical needs. After all, doesn't it make sense to seek out the best professionals to make sure the last part of their lives aren't financial disasters?

Most people who have achieved financial success have had help. Similarly, hasn't every athlete who has won a professional championship or an Olympic medal had a coach? Even with all the technical sophistication and training aids available, the greatest athletes still rely on their coaches to observe, instruct and help them reach their full potential. The world's best golfers regularly seek instruction from specialists. They spend huge amounts of money to have someone help them make the smallest, almost undetectable change in their swing. They spend equal amounts just to have someone watch them putt. Putt! A movement of the shoulders and arms that is perhaps 24 inches from start to finish, yet the world's best golfers need someone to watch them make that smallest of body movements and tell them what they can do to improve.

Our Broker-Dealer sponsored the USA Women's Bobsledding Team at the last Olympics. Did anyone suggest that team go to the Olympics without their coach? Of course not. And yet, how much have the rules or techniques of bobsledding changed in the last 100 years? I don't mean to oversimplify, but essentially you jump on a rolling sled, keep your head down, and try not to fall off. If you don't crash into a snow bank, you might win. It's not that complicated; but most people will agree you need expert coaching if you expect to win a medal. Michael Jordan is another great example. He was generally regarded as the greatest basketball player of all time, yet he wasn't good enough to make his high school team. He learned to play better and more consistently from his coaches – men who could not jump as high or shoot as well, but they taught him what he needed to learn to become great. He listened because he realized he couldn't achieve his dream without help.

The help you receive from a caring advisor is not limited to technical expertise. Much of what you must learn to be successful relates to attitude adjustments and behavior modifications. It's important to accept the fact that you are not smarter than the people who make a living doing this. You are not going to beat them at their own game, just as you are not going to walk into a professional poker tournament and come out the champion. Yes, it happens every light year or so, but those are not the odds you want when it comes to your financial future.

Instead, every decision you make along the way must be driven by a solid plan. If you don't have a process that is systematic, unemotional and diversified, there's little hope of attaining the best results. A coach can help you be the best you can be, but you must be willing to play the game. To reach your potential, you must make the necessary sacrifices, accept coaching and get in the game. You need to step up to the plate and be willing to make mistakes so your coach can help you improve.

Just as a good sports coach can help you get the best results from whatever skills you have, a good financial coach can help you recognize your weaknesses and maximize your strengths. But it must all start with you; the coach is merely a facilitator. You must take personal responsibility for your own success. The best athletes in the world can't be helped if they are unwilling to make necessary changes in their habits and attitude. It takes time and effort and, often, won't feel natural. It wasn't easy for Michael Jordan, Joe Montana or Mary Lou Retton to rise to the pinnacle of their sport. Yet they were willing to accept criticism and coaching. They had the determination to be the best they could be and the discipline to pay the price for success. Whatever sacrifices were involved, none of them quit because it was too difficult.

The same holds true in striving for financial success. Most people would rather spend than save. It takes discipline to change. It takes energy and commitment to create a better future for you and your family.

Objectivity and Independence

When seeking a financial coach to help you, it's important to find one who is independent, unbiased and willing to become your financial shepherd. Granted, virtually every advisor *claims* to be independent, and they may even believe it. When I was new in the financial services business, I believed I was independent because that's what my company's management told me. But like many advisors, I was living in a little cave, my professional world, restricted by what my company told me was the truth. Once I left my company cave and became truly independent, I was exposed to a whole universe of new financial products and strategies. It was a revelation, and it took me the better part of a year to learn about all the things I didn't know existed, despite being one of the company's top producers nationally. You should never work with an advisor who is restricted to the products he or she can offer you or is obliged to meet a sales quota.

When selecting a financial coach, keep in mind that what makes the most money for brokers does not necessarily make the most money for their clients. For example, transactions make the most money for brokers, and may make clients feel good because they believe they are doing something positive. Unfortunately, when conditions are at their worst, people often feel compelled to react. However, experience teaches us that oftentimes the best thing to do when the markets are at their worst is to remain calm, assess the situation and do nothing or do nothing more than rebalance.

By answering the questions on Chart 8.1 (below), you will have a better idea whether or not your financial advisor is truly suited to look after your financial needs.

Chart 8.1 HIRING A FINANCIAL COACH

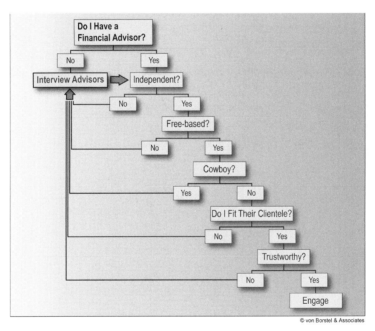

© von Borstel & Associates

My job is to get clients to do the right thing, even though intuitively, it may not be what they want to do. It may not be what a broker is telling their neighbors to do, and it certainly isn't what the Wall Street marketers are telling them they must do; but it is often the right thing for the client because what I suggest to them is based on independent analysis.

That's the value of having an advisor who is an advocate, a shepherd, and not a cowboy. Independent advisors take satisfaction from doing the right thing for their clients. They put their client's needs first. Some will tell you they have a secret formula or product to make you rich without sacrifice. Just like the wonder diets, they usually don't work, but they sure sell. The secret is no secret at all. You must do things the right way: have a process, be systematic, unemotional and diversified. You must focus on achieving your goals and accept that you must make some financial sacrifices en route.

A current advertisement for a stock trading system is the quintessential example of financial pornography. It claims, "You will know exactly when to get in and when to get out of the market."

Ninety-nine percent of what people hear regarding investing is based on emotion and the myth that financial success can be achieved without pain. Again, the truth is hard to hear. It may be convoluted and hard to explain, and it often doesn't feel quite right, emotionally. A good coach knows it must be repeated and re-explained, and that takes time and patience.

Along with finding an advisor who is both independent and willing to tell you what you need to hear, you also should seek an advisor whose client base is similar to you. An example of why this is important is if you have a portfolio of a few hundred thousand dollars, and the advisor's clients are primarily multi-millionaires, you are likely to get lost in the shuffle.

In recent years, I brought in younger advisors to my practice because I knew I could not continue to give my best efforts to more than a few hundred clients or to a client base widely divergent in wealth. Today, my associates and I each devote our efforts to a specific group of clients with similar needs and wealth profiles. It allows us to grow the practice while helping clients in varying circumstances and has proven to be the best situation for all concerned. This has allowed me to only accept clients in whose lives I believe I can make a significant difference.

Let me reiterate the three things that I believe will ultimately determine whether you achieve the level of financial success you want:

- Find an independent, capable coach to help you through the necessary processes.

- Adopt a winning attitude. You must decide whether to listen or ignore the advice you receive, whether to save or spend, to be prudent or chase returns, and to decide whether to sit on the sidelines or get in the game.

- Take action.

Remember, the best athletes in the world perform better with professional coaching. The same is true for retirement planning and investing. No matter what you have achieved in your career, you will not play the retirement game as well alone as you will with a competent advisor. Find a coach to help you be as effective as possible.

Your Legacy

Once you become more financially effective you are in a position that you can give back to others in need, those who are not as fortunate as you. You might give the extra money to children who have virtually nothing. You can build schools, a church, help the homeless, support wounded veterans, plant trees or do whatever you like that will leave the world a better place for you having lived. The more you do for others, the better your life becomes and the greater your happiness and peace. People who do for others are usually amazed at what they receive in return. Their lives become more full, more purposeful.

What do you want to do for others? What do you want your legacy to be? It doesn't have to be a grandiose statement; it can be something less ambitious. Perhaps something only you and your family knows about, such as making sure your grandchildren can attend college or have a down payment for their first home. The smartest and most successful among us often can't see the trees because we are in the forest. A coach can take us out of the forest, out of our box so we can see the possibilities.

Challenge yourself! As a successful person, you have probably overcome challenges in your careers and personal life, so why not finish the job by getting help to do the best you can and create the greatest impact you can? A great coach can help you plan better, achieve more, do more good, and have a more fulfilling life with less stress and confusion.

Include your spouse in your coaching sessions and, when appropriate, other members of your family. I've seen untold instances where a husband dies and the surviving spouse has no idea of what to do with the estate because the husband made all the financial decisions. Together you should make the decision as to how you are going to make a difference. That way, if one of you is no longer here, the other one can carry on your legacy.

Again, it's important to review your estate plan from a holistic perspective to see if your documents are correct and accurately reflect your wishes. Errors or missing elements could result in your beneficiaries getting less than you wanted them to, family members going to war with one another or unanticipated tax nightmares being triggered.

An Educated Advisor

An advisor's intellectual capital is a critical element for clients to consider when selecting a competent and caring advisor. It requires time and commitment for an advisor to participate in peer group conferences and industry forums. The benefits include connecting with like-minded experts in other areas of financial services, keeping abreast of product enhancements and innovations, finding alternative solutions to complex financial issues, and forming affiliations with complementary service providers. An advisor's clients can benefit from all of these.

I belong to financial study groups in several areas of the country. In Oregon, I've been a member of a professional study group for nearly two decades. We meet regularly to discuss issues we face in helping clients deal with the continuously evolving financial and regulatory environment. I also belong to a group in Florida that is dedicated to helping clients who come into sudden wealth, including widows, divorcees, professional athletes and lottery winners.

I joined these groups to gain outside perspectives so I could become a better advisor and help clients become the best they can be. The interaction with other informed financial professionals improves my decision-making, analytical capabilities and thought processes. And, by forming associations with other successful advisors and financial professionals, I often find solutions to problems that fall outside my area of expertise. This gives my clients access to additional resources in situations where I may not have the best answer to a specific problem.

It's virtually impossible to keep current with every nuance and change to financial products. Utilizing the help of other industry professionals who are experts in specific areas has allowed me to contribute to my growing intellectual capital. By having access to these professionals, who can help when needed, I don't have to be an expert on everything to serve my clients. No one in financial services knows it all. If they tell you they do, they don't know much.

When I started in this industry, I thought I knew most everything I needed to know. I trusted that people who were mentoring me knew it all as well; but they didn't. I've since found that the more I learn, the more I realize there is so much more to know. That's why the intellectual capital around me can help me deal with whatever issues I encounter. With these valuable associations, I can truly help people solve their problems and reach their goals.

Why I Do What I Do

When I go to church I like to hear a sermon that makes me think. If, instead, I only hear stories from the pulpit that make me feel good, what is the benefit? A good sermon forces me to confront my shortcomings and helps me gradually change so I will live a better life and make better decisions.

The same is true of financial advice. Once in awhile, we all need a fire and brimstone sermon that yanks us out of our comfort zone and challenges us with out-of-the-box thinking. We have to move outside our little box so we can get a better view of it, maybe realize it is not what we thought it was, then get back in the box and deal with reality.

I love helping people see the reality of their circumstances, or their box if you will. Clients talk at great length with me about their lives, fears and ambitions, and about the things that are most important to them. They let me into their hearts and their financial closets. They let me become their devil's advocate. It is an enormous responsibility, and I am constantly aware that if I say the wrong thing they may slam the door on me, no longer allowing me to help them repair their situations. That is the risk I am willing to take to get close to my clients. I find the potential reward of helping people change their lives is well worth it.

Sometimes it is difficult for a client to talk about their financial issues and how they affect their personal lives, relationships with family and friends, and their ability to simply take a breath and relax. However, it's important that you find someone you can trust enough to let him or her in and really know who you are, what you treasure and what you fear. It requires profound, personal conversations about the meaning of money.

Most people deal with money the way they do because of their past experiences and upbringing. Many people form their attitudes about money in their early years, watching how their parents handled money or from the circumstances surrounding their first job. These early impressions are powerful and are usually the reasons why people act and respond as they do regarding money. Many find it difficult to examine these attitudes and question whether they are true or appropriate in their current circumstances.

How people regard money plays a major role in what kind of person they are and how they go about their lives. Not many are able to let someone else see them as they really are by having deep discussions. Most would rather maintain the image they have created of how they want others to perceive them. They hide behind that image and protect it. To help them find peace and purpose, I have to find a way to get past that shield so they can open up and see themselves as they really are. That takes trust and time. Few advisors ever get to that place with their clients because they don't see adequate reimbursement for the time invested.

As difficult as it may be for clients to openly communicate on these topics, I believe that if I am truthful with them, together we can reach their goals. It may take several years, especially if they have severe financial concerns, but eventually they will think and do things differently. They will make better choices, and eventually they will arrive at a place they need to be, a place they would never be without having the truth presented to them and a guide to help them along the path.

As my client's financial coach, I help them face reality and make tough decisions. We discuss and evaluate everything that has an impact on their personal lives – everything from their families, careers, aspirations, hobbies and values, to their vacations. I listen to what they want to do, but I am also candid and do what is necessary to protect them financially. I strive to remove their fears about the future and give them the tools to be successful. Whether they use the tools or I do, it does not matter as long as they thrive and grow.

I strive to make sure each decision we make during my client's accumulation period will bring them closer to reaching a successful retirement. If they learn the rules of the game of life, they can win.

As you move through your financial life, be mindful that it is a long season and you probably won't win every game. You may get knocked down and hurt occasionally, but that is part of being in the game. What is important is whether you have the confidence that you will eventually win and the resiliency to get up again if you are down. If you do that, and maintain a positive attitude, you have a good chance of winning.

Everyone has different capabilities. That's why it is important that you focus on doing the best you can with what you have been given. What others do should not affect what you do, because your talents, objectives, weaknesses and capacities are different from theirs. The key to winning the game is to play the most prudent, efficient, positive game you can with what you have.

My commitment to my clients is to help them be the best they can be. It's why I do what I do.

◆◆◆